The Power Of Choice

Inviting Freedom and Miracles into Your Everyday Life

By
Lindsay Tallarita

Copyright © 2019 by Lindsay Tallarita

All rights reserved. This book or any portion thereof may not be reproduced or used in any manner whatsoever without the express written permission of the publisher except for the use of brief quotations in a book review.

Printed in the United States of America

First Printing, 2019

ISBN (Paperback): 978-1-947837-07-2

ISBN (Hardback): 978-1-947837-08-9

www.lindsaytallarita.com

Scripture quotations marked (NIV) are taken from the Holy Bible, New International Version®, NIV®. Copyright © 1973, 1978, 1984, 2011 by Biblica, Inc.™ Used by permission of Zondervan. All rights reserved worldwide. www.zondervan.com The "NIV" and "New International Version" are trademarks registered in the United States Patent and Trademark Office by Biblica, Inc.™

Scripture quotations marked (ESV) are from the ESV® Bible (The Holy Bible, English Standard Version®), copyright © 2001 by Crossway Bibles, a publishing ministry of Good News Publishers. Used by permission. All rights reserved.

Scripture quotations marked (NLT) are taken from the Holy Bible, New Living Translation, copyright ©1996, 2004, 2015 by Tyndale House Foundation. Used by permission of Tyndale House Publishers, a Division of Tyndale House Ministries, Carol Stream, Illinois 60188. All rights reserved.

Scripture quotations marked (NKJV) taken from the New King James Version®. Copyright © 1982 by Thomas Nelson. Used by permission. All rights reserved.

Scripture quotations marked (NASB) taken from the New American Standard Bible® (NASB), Copyright © 1960, 1962, 1963, 1968, 1971, 1972, 1973, 1975, 1977, 1995 by The Lockman Foundation. Used by permission. www.Lockman.org.

My 2019 Declaration: I resolve to keep going and live.

Let us hold unswervingly to the hope we profess, for he who promised is faithful.

Hebrews 10:23, New International Version[1]

You need to persevere so that when you have done the will of God, you will receive what he has promised.

Hebrews 10:36, NIV[2]

---

1. *The Holy Bible, New International Version*, (NIV). 2011. Grand Rapids, MI. Zondervan Publishing House.
2. *The Holy Bible, New International Version,* (NIV). 2011. Grand Rapids, MI. Zondervan Publishing House.

September 10th, 2016

God,

I want this to be Your book, for Your glory, to free people. In all things, I want everything in my life to point to You and Your miraculous power to save and set free. You gave me this principle of seeing Your power at work in my life. This principle and vision have allowed me to live a life that I never imagined possible, because I am able to see Your hand in my everyday life.

Not a day goes by where I don't see Your hand or hear Your voice, and that didn't happen by accident. I pray these pages are not my words, but Your words. I can write and say a multitude of things, but I've learned it's Your words that move mountains and set captives free. God, please lead me in this journey. I ask that anyone who reads this book draws nearer to You, trusting You in both the small and big things, and for the miraculous in their lives.

Amen.

Contents

Foreword	1
Acknowledgements	5
Preface	7
Chapter 1: My Story	11
Chapter 2: My "Sermon"	17
Chapter 3: The Power of Choice to Surrender	31
Chapter 4: The Power of Choice to Forgive	43
Chapter 5: The Power of Choice to Have Faith	59
Chapter 6: The Power of Choice to Press In	75
Chapter 7: The Power of Choice to Worship	87
Chapter 8: The Power of Choice to Be Thankful	103
Chapter 9: The Power of Choice to Return	117
Chapter 10: The Power of Choice to Obey	129
Chapter 11: The Power of Choice to Persevere	137
Chapter 12: Inviting Miracles into your Everyday Life	149
Resources	159

Foreword

I first met Lindsay Tallarita in January 2015 when she walked through the doors of our St. Louis Mercy Multiplied Home. In her late 20's at the time, Lindsay was already dealing with a lifetime of pain. Life had already thrown Lindsay some of the most difficult things an individual would ever have to face, including her parents battling alcoholism and her mother dying from a prescription drug overdose.

Lindsay's attempts to cope with so much heartache and dysfunction at such a young age led her into a life of self-harm, as she began cutting herself at age 11. Lindsay was verbally, emotionally, and sexually abused in her childhood and early teen years and was raped by a complete stranger at the age of 18. This led to an ongoing struggle with depression, and Lindsay tried to fill the void in her life with sex and alcohol. She felt extremely hopeless and battled constantly with thoughts of suicide. It was also during her teen years that she began to struggle with an eating disorder.

Lindsay first heard about Mercy at a Point of Grace concert, and God later revealed that she had to get help, or she was not going to make it. During the intake process at the end of 2014, Lindsay made this statement to one of our Mercy staff, "I desire a close relationship with God, but I feel that I have disqualified myself due to my life choices."

When Lindsay walked through the doors of our Mercy home a month later, she found out that the name of our counseling model is called, "Choices that Bring Change." While going through the program, Lindsay quickly received a revelation from God that she had the power to make her own choices, and that those choices would bring about great change in her future.

During her time at Mercy, Lindsay learned that she could choose to forgive. She quickly made a total commitment of her life to Christ, and she began to renew her mind to the Word of God. She began to identify the lies that she had believed about herself and her past and even about God, and she replaced those lies with God's Truth. Lindsay quickly realized that the fruit of her own choices was bringing freedom into her own heart and life. Lindsay also received a revelation from God during her time at Mercy that through the power of her choice to choose the life that God had provided for her, that she could start a generation of blessing that would lead to an amazing future.

As the weeks and months flew by, Lindsay experienced deep healing in her heart and in her emotions. She definitely received and experienced the revelation that Jesus came to heal broken hearts and set captives free. After a lifetime of pain and agony, Lindsay was transformed by the power of Christ in the 8 months that she spent at Mercy. She came in hurting and broken, and she left experiencing great freedom because of being empowered to choose to live according to God's way. Since graduating from Mercy in 2015, Lindsay has continued to make great choices and to grow deeper and stronger in her relationship with Christ.

I cannot think of anyone who is more qualified to write a book about how the power of the choices we make bring freedom and miracles into our everyday life. Since graduating in 2015, Lindsay spent 4 years working for Dave Ramsey at Ramsey Solutions in the Nashville area. She also became an active member of her church, Citipointe Church. She serves with the young adults, youth group, and children's ministry. In addition, Lindsay is now leading a Keys to Freedom study with the young adult's group, and she also leads a life group for middle school age girls. I could not be more proud of Lindsay, because I have watched her walk out her freedom as an amazing overcomer of all the things that have happened to her in the past. She continues to make choices that are pleasing to God, and the fruit of her life is evident!!

Nancy Alcorn

Founder & President of Mercy Multiplied

Acknowledgements

Thank you to Nancy Alcorn, the founder of Mercy Multiplied. Your walk of faith has been used by God to set thousands of women free, and many more thousands to come. I will never stop being grateful for your obedience to where God called you– and the faith to walk it out! I am labeling you a "freedom-bringer." My dream is for God to use me as a freedom-bringer to others as well. You inspire me to become all God has me to be.

Thank you, Mercy staff, for loving me unconditionally by the power of Jesus. Thank you for loving me in the dark and messy moments and helping me to fight for my life. To my Mercy counselor, Katie McPhee, I am grateful that you never gave up on me and walked with me through the process. I now have the tools I need to seek God with all my life and heart, and the same God that saved me, keeps me.

Thank you, Kristin Lea, for sharing your personal story and encouragement while I was a resident at Mercy. Learning about your raw, hard moments and how God used your faith to perform miracles gave me the faith to trust for my own. I went from thinking running was crazy and torturous to pushing myself harder than I ever had before. I developed a new passion and learned a lesson from God along the way.

I want to say a special thank you to Melanie Harbert, the program director of Mercy Multiplied in St. Louis, Missouri. Without you encouraging me to ask God what my personal "sermon" would be, this book would have never been in existence. On the last day of my 5K training at Mercy, I'll never forget being so excited to share with you the vision God gave me. That vision keeps me walking in freedom today. You are such an incredible woman of God, and I was so blessed by your leadership in the Mercy home. What you do matters so much more than I could ever express with words.

I also want to say thank you to my friends, family, and professionals around the globe who also never gave up on me, even when I wanted to give up on me. To my friends here in Nashville, thank you for encouraging me and being a part of this book coming to fruition. I needed all your prayers, pep talks, and butt-kicking along the way!

Most of all, thank you to my Heavenly Father. Thank you for life. Thank you for strength. Thank you for dreams. Thank you for hope.

Preface

I have been trying to start this book for the past four years. Various obstacles kept me from truly committing to begin this work. I won't go through all the challenges I faced and excuses I made, but overcoming the fear of writing this book was a giant leap for me. When I made my very first outline, I started to experience major pushback from Satan, and I wondered if I was ready to write this at all. I know I will never arrive at perfection when it comes to the principles in this book, but I started to question if I was the one who was supposed to write down what God was teaching me. I asked myself, "Am I even qualified to write this? Who am I to speak into another person's power of choice?"

As I asked myself those questions, I had no idea I was about to face another challenging season; one when God spoke into my qualification and affirmed that He has equipped and chosen me to share this message. As I faced a new battle with an autoimmune disease, I wondered if my belief in God's vision was strong enough to persevere through spiritual, emotional, mental, and physical pain. In this trial, I would find that my belief was secure– it would even help me to overcome the sickness and chronic physical pain. This trying season was a deepening of faith, and left me ready to share this.

In the midst of the discouragement I experienced from the disease and physical pain, I chose to continue pressing into God, and He showed up. He revealed to me the reason behind Satan's attacks. Satan wanted me to believe that I could not overcome this new challenge because he did not want this book written. He is terrified of what could happen as I release this book in obedience. I believe this message will help you to believe in God and to achieve greater feats than you have dared to imagine. That scares Satan to the core of his being. God showed up, and I showed up, and I am so excited to share this book with you.

This book examines the power of choices in our lives. These require decision, action, and movement. It is easy for someone who has had very little resistance in their life to lecture about choices, but that's not my history. God has brought me through the darkest of depths, and I know that my story is what qualifies me to tell you about your power of choice. This book is not written to invalidate your pain, your illness, or your struggles. I know firsthand that they are very real and can cause you to feel like you have absolutely no choices or control in your life. That was my belief once too.

This book is about both God's power and our power of choice. We will witness what is released into the spiritual and physical world when those two powers meet. I lived believing that I did not have a choice in anything in my life. I felt that I had to do whatever good or bad things people wanted me to do. I had no choice in the way I thought or talked about myself. I remember explaining to a counselor that I felt like I had a filter on my brain that only let me see, think, and believe negative things. The good felt like it could not get through, no matter how hard I tried to find it. I also felt I had no choice in speaking up. My voice did not matter, and when I did try to use it, it seemed that I could only judge and condemn myself.

The amazing thing is that those negative beliefs and words were not the ultimate truth. They were only what I felt. Those lies stemmed from what I experienced as a child and grew to become my core beliefs about myself as an adult. I walked through my days lifeless, unknowingly trying to find either death or true life. You can only live this way in your own strength for so long before exhausting, paralyzing, and destroying yourself.

When reading the words and choices presented in this book, ask God to show you where you can apply this to your life. Ask Him to guide you to truth and what He has for you. The hardness and pain you may currently be experiencing in your life is real. However, I believe that this pain is an opportunity. God has so many miracles He wants you to see right before your very eyes. I've seen firsthand that God can take our brokenness and bring about hope and beauty. No matter what storms may come or how hopeless you feel, I pray God would strengthen our faith to trust Him for a lifetime of freedom and miraculous moments.

Chapter 1

My Story

I can hardly wait to share the vision God has given me about how to see miracles in your life, but first, I want to share a bit of my story and heart behind this book. I am a Mercy Multiplied graduate, and prior to my time at Mercy, living was an impossible task for me. Mercy Multiplied is a faith-based organization and residential facility that helps girls and women overcome many types of life controlling issues and learn how to live a life of freedom. Some of the life controlling issues Mercy is equipped to handle include: eating disorders, addictions, self-harm, abuse, sexual assault, and human trafficking. From the early age of eleven, I was constantly suicidal. I lived knowing any day, month, or year could be the time I succeeded at tragically ending my life. Annually, I updated my suicide note and goodbye letters that I wanted to leave behind for family and friends. Perhaps this was because I was told by multiple people that suicide was a selfish thing, so I wanted to do whatever I could to make sure it was "less" selfish. At least three of my high school classmates committed suicide, and the hardest thing for me to grasp was that I hadn't realized the intense level of pain they carried. I personally have a hard time with things that don't make sense or still feel unfinished. Maybe it's not just me, maybe more people out there feel that way too.

In the journey I had with depression, anxiety, and suicide, I was labeled with more mental illnesses than I knew what to do with. Doctors diagnosed me with major depressive disorder, generalized anxiety disorder, panic disorder, post-traumatic stress disorder, seasonal affective disorder, borderline personality disorder, and bipolar disorder– you get the picture. My mind was an intensely dark place. I'm sure I'd be shocked to see the doctor's additional notes on my medical charts; there was probably even more that they chose not to tell me.

I tried everything the mental health world had to offer to find freedom. I did medications, psychiatry, counseling, therapy groups, and both inpatient and outpatient hospitalizations, but nothing truly made me want to live. I would sometimes see improvement for a few days, and on rare occasions, a few weeks. I can count the number of times on one hand that I felt stable for a whole month. The improvement and relief I experienced were always temporary. Please know that I'm not bashing the mental health world or what it offers. It kept me alive for another day many times. Some of the medications did end up having side effects that harmed me more than helped, but I also know that without the help I received I would not have been able to survive. Eventually, I simply came to realize that these diagnoses and prescriptions could never set me free. Nevertheless, I am grateful that they did keep me alive long enough for Jesus to liberate me.

The darkness that hung over me, spanning from my childhood all the way to my adulthood, came from unresolved trauma and pain. It took me a long time to realize that it is not normal for a kid to wake up one day and decide she wants to die. As a child, the depression felt like my fault. I believed it was something that was wrong with me, like a part of my human character flaws. To cope with the darkness within, I started starving and harming myself. Starving myself gave me a sense of control and the ability to feel small, almost hidden from life. Cutting myself felt like I was somehow releasing the pain that was stuck inside of me. Those addictions only brought me more pain, shame, and suffering.

When I found Jesus just before my eighteenth birthday, it was my very first glimmer of something better. Right away in my relationship with God, I knew that Jesus meant hope. However, when I didn't see my darkness immediately vanish, I assumed the answer was to just try harder, be better, and hide the struggles. I kept failing again and again. I had suddenly received this new title of "Christian," and while my relationship with God was very real and important to me, I couldn't find the abundance and new life He talked about. I didn't see chains breaking or freedom arriving. I only heard lies. At the time, I didn't even know they were lies. I knew them to be reality and my truth.

I wasn't worthy.
I wasn't enough.
I wasn't special.
I didn't matter.
I was too much.
I was needy.
I was broken.
I was unimportant.
I was ugly.
I was bad.
I was dirty.
I was shameful.
I was stupid.
I was alone.
I was unloved.
I was messy.
I was dramatic.
I was unpopular.
I was unwanted.

I hated myself, I hated who I was, and I hated my body. The negative voices in my mind consumed my attention, and every painful experience I lived through seemed to confirm my worthlessness. As much as I tried in my own strength to want to live, I couldn't. I often tell people the most painful thing I have ever been through in life is living each day wanting to die. As emotionally painful as sexual abuse and other hardships were, they were nothing compared to the pain of waking up every day, going on living and breathing while wanting to die. The only conclusion I could come to was that God somehow didn't create me with the ability to survive.

Trauma and abuse can cause you to believe and experience moments of near insanity. Spending decades trying to escape and numb the pain finally built up to an explosion. This was a catastrophic season in my life where I destroyed everything I could lay my hands on. After spending months devouring alcohol and as many men in hotel rooms as I could get, I no longer could even recognize myself in a mirror. I remember sitting in my car one night, hating myself more than I ever thought possible because of how my toxic behavior had hurt another broken person. I hunched in my seat, looking in the car mirror, screaming to my own reflection about how horrible I was and sobbing hysterically. I was hopeless and I wanted to die.

Thankfully, even in the midst of a suicide attempt, that's not where my story ended. God led me to apply for Mercy Multiplied. It was at Mercy that I began to recognize the lies for what they were and learned how to replace them with God's truth. God started to show me who He really created me to be, and repeatedly spoke of His character and love for me. My time at Mercy was one of the hardest things I have ever had to do, because I had to face the abuse and demons from my past. It took me months to see how God was healing and transforming me. Through training for my first 5K race at Mercy, God showed me *how* I was beginning to see and experience those miracles in both the spiritual and physical realms.

Now I am a completely different person.
I am new.
I am redeemed.
I am transformed.
I am worthy.
I am beautiful.
I am seen.
I am treasured.
I am loved.
I am set free.
I am healed.
I am whole.
I am strong.
I am enough.
I am talented.
I am creative.
I am kind.
I am alive.
I am grateful.
I am courageous.
I matter.
I want to live.
I love life.
I love deeply.
I have faith.

I have joy.
I have hope.
I have dreams.
I can trust.
I can believe.
I am gentle and passionate.
I am fierce and tenderhearted.
In Christ, there is nothing that is impossible for me.

Here's the beautiful thing, dear friend: in Christ, there is nothing that is impossible for you. Whatever lies you are struggling with, or situations that seem hopeless, we all can bring those burdens to the feet of Jesus. God's goodness and power are more infinite than we could ever truly imagine, and these following chapters will help you to see the choices God invites us to make as we see the impossible become possible in our lives. I am so excited for this journey together. God has a beautiful and an abundant life for you, full of freedom and miracles. This is my inheritance, and it's yours too.

If you, or someone you know are a female age 13-32, and have a life controlling issue, go to www.mercymultiplied.com for help and more information.

Chapter 2

My "Sermon"

I was never a runner. In fact, if people ever used race or running scriptures and metaphors, they always clarified with me, "Well, I know you don't really run, but you know what I mean!" I tried a few times to train for 5k races, and it always felt impossible. Beyond just hard work, it felt quite literally impossible. As I look back, that feeling now makes sense. My body had lived in a constant survival mode for years because of the eating disorder. In high school I was reprimanded because I didn't stand during choir practice. Honestly, I physically couldn't. Even in my first weekend at Mercy Multiplied, I felt my physical limitations. Several of us decided to play basketball, and two minutes into the game I collapsed and scraped my knees because I felt so weak. I was prone to giving up with anything in life that felt challenging or involved resistance. Clearly, running was impossible and out of the question.

As God was spiritually, emotionally, and physically healing me in my time at Mercy, I learned that we would have the opportunity to participate in a Mercy 5K. Even though my experiences pointed to the fact that I could never be a runner, something stirred inside of me. It felt impossible, but I was also beginning to see glimpses of God doing the impossible in my life. Could it be possible? Could this girl who spent her life starving and harming her body ever cross the finish line? I began to let myself wonder, grabbing onto that glimmer of hope.

The training seemed so minimal, but I was amazed to see progress as I kept following the training plan! I began running for one minute, which became ninety seconds, somehow climbing to three minutes, then five, and even more. As I was nearing the end of my training, I realized God was teaching me a lesson in perseverance. I was ecstatic to share that lesson with several of the staff members at Mercy, and before the final day of training, I was encouraged to ask God on that run what "my sermon" would be. Mel, the program director, said it might not be a message for a rapt audience, but maybe just for my own heart. That didn't matter– I should ask either way. I was amazed by what God showed me while I was running 3.1 miles that day. As much as I love simple processes and steps, life continues to show me that it is not just all about orderly outlines or ABCs. There is so much we journey through and discover along the way that can't be put in a box. Still, God knows that simple processes speak to my heart. He gave me an equation that day which has shaped the way I trust God with miracles in my life.

God's Infinite Power + The Power Of Our Choice

=

Seeing Freedom, The Impossible, And Miracles In Everyday Life.

As God gave this equation to me, it wasn't about a new formula to pursue. It was Him showing me how I was already seeing so many impossible things become possible in my life. I was in awe of what He showed me, because it pointed to His sovereignty and goodness in my life. This revelation also helped me to make sense of the role that I play as the recipient and participant in those miracles. Together, let's break down a few ideas in this equation.

Miracles

Let's begin with the end result: visibly seeing freedom, the impossible, and miracles in our lives. I believe miracles are happening every moment all around us. There are big ones; like when you're staring at a bottle of pills and out of nowhere a friend calls and tells you she's been praying for you. Milestones such as hearing your cousin has been shot in the head four times, yet they somehow survived. Moments like when you've done the chemo, done the surgery, and are declared cancer free. Miracles when you've been told you will never walk again... and then your feet regain their steps. These types of miracles leave us in the utmost gratitude, knowing that only God could move such an immense mountain.

On the other hand, there are smaller miracles. Littler marvels may not change your belief systems or worldview, but they somehow still speak life and hope to your heart. Maybe that's a day you leave work in tears, wondering how you'll ever measure up to being enough, and then "that song," the one that gently restores your heart, plays on the radio. It could be a smile on a child's face as they splash through a rainy day. What are those small miracles for you?

For me these days, it's when I'm in a time of stress and God reminds me to take a moment to be still and breathe. In that moment, I taste the sweetness of blueberry honey tea. In that moment, I feel the warmth of sunshine on my face. In that moment, I hear the song of the birds and have a renewed sense that life is all around me. To me, that is freedom and peace in my soul. I believe these are the moments that speak to the word *selah*. This word shows up frequently in the Psalms, and I've heard many pastors speak into its meaning. What I've gathered is this: when God is instructing us to *selah*,

He is asking us to take a moment and ponder, to breathe His presence and what He is saying in that moment. He wants us to press into times of *selah* to see and experience His goodness, and to breathe fresh life into us. Don't miss out on how God wants to use this word of *selah* in your life. Maybe even set down this book for a minute, take a deep breath, and notice how He is surrounding you with His love.

What about the miracles we never even know about? Have you ever thought about those? When I moved to Nashville the end of 2015, one of my favorite prayers became, "God, please fill the gap with your favor." I knew that there were things about my new life that I felt inadequate for, and I was surrounded with situations outside of my control. In those moments, I knew the best thing for me to do was to invite God to fill the gap. I'd ask him to hold that overpacked suitcase together for one more flight. I'd request that He fill in the gap with confidence on this job interview. In times when I'm feeling my neediness for God, I am often reminded that I need God in ways I can't always imagine or see. However, there are also times when I feel secure and stable, often unaware to the possibility of miracles surrounding me. I still need Him to fill the gap when I feel good and secure, even if I don't recognize it. In Psalm 91, it says that when the LORD is our refuge, He will command His angels concerning us to guard us in all our ways. The Hebrew-Greek Keyword Study Bible describes the Hebrew word for command as an order and commission, stating that *"His commands are unique, requiring an inner commitment, not merely external, superficial obedience."* That means when God commands His angels to us, their inner commitment is to protect and guard us.[3]

---

3. *Hebrew-Greek Keyword Study Bible*, New International Version. 1996. Chattanooga, TN. AMG International, INC, 696, 1546.

Wow, doesn't that make you stop and think? That He commands angels to guard us! Sometimes I wonder how many more car accidents I could have been in without angels. Even if you're a perfect driver (who I have yet to meet), what about icy, rainy, or snowy days? What about those that are distracted driving around me, let alone if I reach to grab my tea, put on some lip gloss, or change the radio station? Unfortunately, I've been in a few car accidents, but when I stop and think about the variables, I'm shocked that I've made it home safe each day. I'm not a theology expert, and I can't tell you why some days I feel like I've been more protected than others, but I can tell you I truly believe angels have stepped in and intervened on God's behalf when a normal everyday moment could have turned disastrous.

Known or unknown, big or small, miracles are always happening. I'm grateful even for the one's I can't see, and I long for my faith to see more of these miracles played out in my life daily. I have found such delight, awe, and wonder in seeing the miracles God performs, and even better, the deep gratitude I feel seeps into the deepest places of my soul. That gratitude burns away doubt and grows the seed of belief that God sees me and loves me more than I could ever fully comprehend.

Maybe we could sit with that majestic idea for a minute. He sees me. He sees me when I'm in the midst of a belly laugh because of a surprise from a friend. He sees me as I recount the day, wondering if I did enough. He sees me when the pain is so intense, and I wonder if the only option for relief is to rip my heart out. In every day, He sees me. Because I am a writer, I love words. That shouldn't surprise you! In my personal Bible studies, I have loved learning the meaning of Greek and Hebrew words, and especially the different names that are used for God and His characteristics. Hagar may not be one of the most popular women of the Bible, but I love studying the interactions between her and God in Genesis 16, where El Roi, the God who sees, shows up.

To set the scene, Abram, Sarai, and Hagar have a messy relationship. Abram, who is later renamed Abraham, walked with God by faith. Like us, he traveled on an imperfect journey with mistakes along the way. While Abram and Sarai were awaiting the child God promised them despite infertility, Abram took matters into his own hands and slept with Hagar. When Hagar realized she was pregnant with Abram's child, the dysfunctional cycle in their relationship intensified. Hagar became prideful about her pregnancy and made sure Sarai knew that, which in turn Sarai used as a reason to mistreat Hagar. Due to this mistreatment, Hagar ran away and fled into the desert. Put yourself in Hagar's place for a moment. I can imagine her, hurt and discouraged from the mistreatment and mixed messages. She was pregnant and alone, and fear must have been gripping her heart. This is where the God who sees steps into the scene.

> *And he said, "Hagar, slave of Sarai, where have you come from, and where are you going?" "I'm running away from my mistress Sarai," she answered. Then the angel of the LORD told her, "Go back to your mistress and submit to her." The angel added, "I will increase your descendants so much that they will be too numerous to count." The angel of the LORD also said to her: "You are now pregnant, and you will give birth to a son. You shall name him Ismael, for the LORD has heard your misery. He will be a wild donkey of a man; his hand will be against everyone and everyone's hand against him, and he will live in hostility toward all his brothers." She gave this name to the LORD who spoke to her: "You are the God who sees me," for she said, "I have now seen the One who sees me."*
> *(NIV, Verses 8-14)*[4]

---

4. *The Holy Bible, New International Version*, (NIV). 2011. Grand Rapids, MI. Zondervan Publishing House.

Hagar encountered the God who sees that day. Although Hagar's son was not the promised one, God still met her where she was and spoke into her life. I don't know about you, but when I feel seen by God, that moment is a miracle to me. When He sees me in the broken moments, I feel loved and cared for. When He sees me in the joyful moments, I also feel loved and grateful.

He loves me. He loves me when I bring chicken noodle soup to my sick neighbors. He loves me when I sponsor a child in need. He loves me when I turn my back and run away. He loves me when I turn back, wondering how I let my sin take me so far. He loves me always. I want more awareness of that. More of the awe and wonder His love stirs up in me. More delight and gratitude, more knowing He sees me and that He loves me. His love is happening all around, in every moment. Have you realized this incredible truth in your life? Wherever you are in your miracle journey and relationship with God, rest assured that He does in fact see you and know you right where you are.

God's Power

There's so much to be said about God's power. His power is the source of miracles and every good thing. He's the one who has moved mountains and parted seas. He's the God who raised the dead and opened blind eyes. Our God created the universe with the power of His voice and words. In the book *Sparkling Gems from the Greek 2*, author Rick Renner talks about one of the Greek words used for the word "miracles." This term, "dunamis," portrays miracles as an explosive and dynamic power.[5] This type of power I see all over scripture

---
5. Rick Renner, *Sparkling Gems from the Greek Volume II: 365 New Gems to Equip and Empower you for Victory Every Day of the Year*. 2016. Tulsa, OK. Institute Books, 111

as I read the stories of the Bible. While God can and often does use people in these miracles, the source of the power comes from Him. In my recent quiet times with God, I've been reading from the book of Exodus. I've been so excited to reread this book because God showed me the miracles I experienced at Mercy Multiplied were my Exodus. After God rescued the Israelites from Egypt, they were called to remember how God had saved them and set them free from bondage and slavery. God did many miracles for them after that moment, but the deliverance from Egypt is one that was continually recalled in later scriptures. I also have experienced many miracles since Mercy, yet Mercy will always be a miracle I go back to and choose to bring to remembrance.

God made a way in my life where there was no way. He rescued me and set me free from my own version of bondage and slavery. Each day as I've been reading Exodus, God is illuminating different verses and speaking fresh insights in my life. What stands out to me the most in this season is that as God was bringing the Israelites out of slavery, they followed God's leading through Moses, but God is clearly the source of the miracles. In the New Living Translation, verse 3 of chapter 6 says, "This is a day to remember forever– the day you left Egypt, the place of your slavery. Today the LORD has brought you out by the power of his mighty hand."[6] Their miracle came from the power of God! Every miracle starts and ends with God being the source. It is the power of God that brings salvation (Romans 1:16 NIV).[7] It is God and His power in us that does more in our lives than we could

---

6. *The Holy Bible, New International Version,* (NIV). 2011. Grand Rapids, MI. Zondervan Publishing House.
7. *The Holy Bible, New International Version,* (NIV). 2011. Grand Rapids, MI. Zondervan Publishing House.

ever imagine (Ephesians 3:20 NIV).[8] We would be nowhere without His power.

Have you ever watched Louie Giglio's sermon "Our God Is Indescribable?" If you haven't, I highly suggest you watch it. What I love about his message is that it forces us to see how small we are (ouch), but how significant and treasured we are by God. My flesh doesn't love to be confronted by the reality of how small and powerless I am– until it is met with the awesome reality that we are treasured by our Creator. The One who made me and you (the small), also made the big (the stars and suns, and galaxies and universe). Although we weren't there to see the creation of the world, all it takes is staring up at the starry night sky, the breathtaking mountains, or the crashing waves to get a glimpse of His power and bigness. I may be small, but I am held in the hands of the One that holds all the power, and who is worthy of all the glory. God holds more power than He exerted in creation, His capabilities reaching beyond the stars and near to us. What about the woman with the issue of blood (Luke 8:43-48)? Isn't that a miracle? We'll come back to that story in a minute.

This year I was able to travel to Israel for the first time. I knew the trip would be life changing, but it was even much more significant than I expected. I now have a passion for the Bible like I've never had before. Experiencing the land of the Bible has made the scriptures come alive. I can almost envision it while I am reading, I have a deeper understanding, and I'm thirsting for more and more of His word and presence. Now when I'm reading my Bible, I have my map of Israel in front of me, along with my travel guide, pictures, notes from the trip, and of course my cup of coffee!

---

8. *The Holy Bible, New International Version*, (NIV). 2011. Grand Rapids, MI. Zondervan Publishing House.

One of the places I visited in Israel is the ancient city of Migdal, the home of Mary Magdalene. To be honest, I set foot in the ancient ruins with little expectation of how this city might impact me, but I left unfettered and more whole than when I entered. I was completely humbled that day, and I learned to let God bless me in the places I don't expect. As I look back on my time in Israel, I'm grateful Migdal was one of the places He chose to make memorable and meaningful for me, as well as for many others who were on the trip. The more I think about it, Mary Magdalene is probably the woman I relate to most in the Bible. Luke 7 has the story of Jesus being anointed by a sinful woman, who some believe was Mary Magdalene. It's such a beautiful story of a woman who was sinful and unworthy because of the life she lived and the choices she had made, but after knowing and experiencing Jesus, she was forever changed. Although the Pharisees and disciples didn't see someone special, Jesus saw love and forgiveness when He looked at this woman.

Then he turned toward the woman and said to Simon, "Do you see this woman? I came into your house. You did not give me any water for my feet, but she wet my feet with her tears and wiped them with her hair. You did not give me a kiss, but this woman, from the time I entered, has not stopped kissing my feet. You did not put oil on my head, but she has poured out perfume on my feet. Therefore, I tell you, her many sins have been forgiven- as her great love has shown. But whoever has been forgiven little loved little." Then Jesus said to her, "Your sins are forgiven" (Luke 7:44-48 NIV)[9]

---

9. *The Holy Bible, New International Version*, (NIV). 2011. Grand Rapids, MI. Zondervan Publishing House.

My heart leaps for joy at this. I have a messy history. I made sinful and degrading choices, and if the world was looking at my past, it would label me unworthy. Nevertheless, because I have been forgiven much, I have a depth of love for Jesus that can never be taken away from me. Many women who have traveled to the church in ancient Migdal have experienced a wave of mercy in their lives like Mary, and I am also one of those women.

Let's go to the story with the woman who had the issue with blood. In this same city of Migdal, home of the sinful woman, there was another little miracle waiting for me. Our tour guide informed us that tradition holds this was also the road where the woman with the issue of blood touched Jesus. All it took was a touch of Jesus' garment for the power to flow through and heal this woman's body. There is now a magnificent painting at this location where they believe the miracle occurred, and as I touched the floor of this place with my hands and prayed, I experienced His power at work in my body. I felt a peace in my physical body and knew God was beginning another miracle in my life.

I play a part in the miracles I experience in life, like placing my hands on the floor and praying when He asks even if it feels silly– and it did at first. It's important to remember, though, that I can never be the source of those miracles. The same was true for this woman who touched Jesus. This woman had to reach out and touch Jesus in faith, but He did the healing work. It is God who is sustaining all things by His powerful Word (see Hebrews 1:3).[10] Only God holds that power. The next time you get a glimpse of His immensity and power, take a moment to let that awe wash over you as you thank Him, the ultimate source of all good things and miracles in your life.

---

10. *The Holy Bible, New International Version*, (NIV). 2011. Grand Rapids, MI. Zondervan Publishing House.

The Power Of Our Choice

This is the final piece of the equation God gave me during training for that first 5K. Honestly, this has been the hardest- and most freeing- part of the equation. What did I, the sexually abused, depressed, and suicidal little girl, ever have a choice in? I had always thought I was a victim of the choices that were forced upon me. What right did I have to say no to men in future relationships? I believed that I had no power to change my thoughts or live anywhere other than the dark pit that surrounded me. When you are stripped of your choices at such a young age, it's easy to live, breathe, believe, and walk in the mindset that you have no choices in life. Perhaps you can relate to this mentality. For others, you were taught you could say no and that you have certain rights. If that's the case, have you seen how your choices can either bring you into deeper bondage or open a flood gate of healing and freedom?

When we make choices that go against God's will or His Word, I don't believe His heart or plan is to make us pay for what we did, but I do believe there are natural consequences to the choices we make. These consequences can bring about bondage in our life. A natural consequence of my choice to starve myself was ulcers. The ways I chose to medicate and numb my pain led to addictions. Sinful choices lead to bondage and slavery, and choices that align us to the will of God lead to miracles and freedom. Because of God's power, I don't believe He *has* to use us to show His glory, but He *chooses* to use us, especially when it comes to new levels of freedom. When we walk out a life of freedom, that choice says volumes to a dying world that desperately needs hope and miracles.

If you are looking to grow as a leader, influencer, father, mother, or solely in your walk with Christ, you need to listen to Ronnie Doss speak. Being around him helps my dreams of the future to come alive because I'm always challenged to act towards those hopes and dreams instead of passively wishing for the future I want. I don't sit passively and then wonder why my dreams never came to fruition. I could write a whole book on the things I've learned from Ronnie's teachings. The most impactful thing I've heard him say regarding our choices is:

> *"God will open the door to the extent that I am willing to do the work."*

Yes, like you, I've experienced things I didn't choose. I didn't ask to be abused. I didn't decide to have an autoimmune disorder. I didn't request to spend most of my life suffocating in darkness– but when I learned what I *could* choose, that's when everything started to change. When I became willing to do the work of finding freedom, that's when God opened the door and brought beauty from ashes, life from death, and light from the darkness.

When God asks us to do things and take an active approach to the choices we make, I believe it is an invitation to take those steps so that we can grow in our relationship with Him. This process allows us to watch Him increase our faith. The power of choice isn't about the power of positivity or finding an inner strength or peace to save myself or create the life I want. It's about lining up my will with the will and power of God. It's crucial that I get myself in agreement with His Truth and Spirit. This path, this choice will allow you to daily experience the freeing presence of God. Let's journey together through several of the choices we do have, that when joined with God's power, will produce freedom in both the big and small miracles of our daily lives.

Chapter 3

The Power of Choice to Surrender

I feel so much better when I have a sense of control. Unfortunately, that control never lasts. Inevitably, at some point, what I think I have control over starts to control me. This chapter has taken months to start, because honestly, I think it's the most frightening. It has certainly required the biggest leap of faith.

When I was eleven, I started struggling with an eating disorder. My chaotic home life left me feeling terrified, unstable, and out of control. Eating, or rather the choice not to eat, was something tangible that was completely in my control. I felt that the more I conquered hunger and resisted food, the more I possessed something no one could take from me. No outside force could make me eat, only my own weakness. That's what I told myself amidst the hunger pains and turmoil.

Control hasn't always looked like an eating disorder. Sometimes it's looked like clinging to a path, person, or idea that I wanted badly enough to do whatever it takes. These behaviors have always led me to confusion, frustration, and anger. I'd ask endless questions: "Why isn't this working?" "What am I doing wrong?" "Is there something wrong with me?" My most famous line in these frustrations is, "Am I crazy?"

As intimidating as surrender sounds, for me, it's always brought relief. Don't get me wrong, it can be incredibly painful. There have been moments of releasing control when I wondered if the ground would open up and the fear would swallow me whole. Nevertheless, whenever I have pushed past that moment, there is a calm that comes with knowing I can't do it all or make all the pieces fit together. In my first several weeks at Mercy Multiplied, the worship leader repeatedly sang the song "Dawn to Dusk" by All Sons and Daughters. The lyrics resonated as we acknowledged, "Today's surrender is tomorrow's freedom." At the time, I had no idea what it meant, but something about that song connected with my heart. I felt compelled to write it down in my journal. Remember that line. We'll be circling back to it later on.

What does surrender look like? What does it mean? For people who know me well, they know my love for definitions and meaning of words. A few definitions that come up for the word surrender:

- To cease resistance and submit to authority
- To give up or hand over
- To abandon oneself entirely[11]

How does that definition make you feel? Are you like me, sensing fear starting to rise? Do you feel excitement and possibility? Does it feel like adventure or punishment to you? I could be speculating, but intuition tells me that for most people, surrender can be frightening. Perhaps it's because there are so many unknowns.

If I don't worry about the doctor's results, will it become my worst fears come to life?

---

11. Surrender. 2019. In *Merriam-Webster.com*. Retrieved July 24, 2019, from https://www.merriam-webster.com/dictionary/surrender.

If I trust that God has a plan for me without trying to control the outcome, can I still receive the desires of my heart?
If I acknowledge that life is hard right now and take a moment to just breathe, will the plates I've been spinning all come crashing down to the ground?

The first time I heard the song "Control" by Tenth Avenue North, I was crying so hard I had to pull over to the side of the road and park. It was a raw moment, and my soul felt thirsty for the words they sang. I encourage you to buy this song and as you listen, let the words wash over you. If you connect with my struggle of giving up control, the song will certainly minister to you. I love how the song reveals God's freeing love that allows us to give Him control.

As a teenager and young adult, surrender was scary because it meant giving up an eating disorder and trusting God to heal the brokenness that led to starving myself. It meant asking God to come into my heart, live there, and then let Him transform me from the inside out. It meant facing the demons from my past and handing them over to God. It's taken me so long to sit and write this chapter because of the reality that I'm still not perfect at surrendering. That imperfection bothers me at times, even though I know it's an unrealistic expectation. So often, I still resist and am tempted to cling tightly to what I want, what feels familiar, and what's comfortable. In the last few years, surrendering has meant acknowledging I'm doing my best and trusting that God will produce the results. It's meant working hard, but not straining and striving, because I can trust God to provide. It still means telling myself every day that God has a plan for my life and is not finished with my story, and that I don't have to be perfect to be accepted or worthy of love. As we consider our choice to surrender, there are three aspects that I've seen at work in my life through the power of choice:

- Surrendering To God's Instruction
- Surrendering To God's Will
- The Product Of Surrender

Surrendering To God's Instruction

Right now, I'm in another new season of surrender that is yet again both scary and exciting. Earlier this year my go-to for daily devotionals each morning was *Sparkling Gems from the Greek 2*. As I shared in the previous chapter, I love studying the Hebrew and Greek words. The January 25th reading spoke to my heart on the importance of surrender:

> *Saying yes to the Lord requires surrender. I'm talking about that moment when you are willing to lay down all your own plans and yield to what the Holy Spirit has revealed to you about God's will for your life. Some people pass this test, whereas others do not. However, those who surrender, yield, and obey experience the joy, power, and victory of the Spirit. They live an enriched life filled both with opportunities to be seized and obstacles to be overcome in order to attain victory and to complete the assignment.*[12]

When I read that earlier this year, I had no idea there would be such a big yes I'd have to say just a few months later. I laugh though when I think about this season, because I

---

12. Rick Renner, *Sparkling Gems from the Greek Volume II: 365 New Gems to Equip and Empower you for Victory Every Day of the Year*. 2016. Tulsa, OK. Institute Books, 97.

technically prayed for it. Isn't it funny how God does that? We pray with a specific outcome in mind, and then are genuinely surprised when the prayer is answered differently than we expected. I think the answer surprises me for two reasons. One, because I often forget there's a process to attaining what I'm asking God for. For example, in 2016, I began to ask God to give me strength. Much to my distress, I realized that just like working out, strength isn't given, it's earned. I began to recognize this when I felt God asking me to pick a word of the year each year. The year I picked the word "strength," I wondered why I felt so weak and attacked in my faith. I soon realized it was because He was not just giving me strength, but something more rich. He was giving me opportunities to grow into a strong person! I had to go through those battles to be given strength. The second reason God's answers surprise me is because I often believe I know the ideal way God could answer my prayers. However, it usually doesn't turn out that way– sometimes it doesn't turn out that way at all.

So here I am, in 2019, my prayer this year being "God, if I am going left in any area of my life, and you want me to go right, speak clearly to me and redirect my steps." If you don't know this about me yet, I am not a huge fan of change. In the past, change to me has meant instability, painful endings, and goodbyes. The fact that I've been open to redirection this year speaks to the level of growth I've experienced. In my newfound boldness, I've learned that not all change is bad, and in fact, most probably isn't. Even when change feels hard, that does not mean it is negative.

When I look back, change has brought some very good and positive things into my life. I'm free because of change. I have a great life in Nashville because of change. While I am growing in my view of change, I wasn't praying this prayer because I was wanting or hoping for some sort of new shift. It was because I want to be so sensitive to the voice of God and his instructions that I'd be willing to surrender and obey, no matter what He is asking. As I write these words, my most recent yes required a scary and painful surrender. At the same time, that choice is exciting and full of so much opportunity. I was outside walking over my lunch break at work, hoping to soak up as much sunshine as I could. As I was walking, I was thinking about this book and my desire to get it into your hands. The last year I've been working to bring this book to completion, and it has brought me so much joy to write. That day, I sensed that God was going to shift things in my life to give me the capacity I needed to finish. The question surprised me, but maybe it won't surprise you after hearing my prayer this year. God spoke to my heart,

"If I asked you to quit your job to finish your book, would you do it?"

I wish I could tell you my answer was simply, "Yes. I surrender. I obey." It wasn't. My response to God was, "Yes, but you are not going to ask me to do that. So, I'm not going to do it." Ouch! I'm sorry, Lord! He took those next 24 hours to correct my response and show me that was what He wanted me to do. Saying yes to God in this path change has required much faith, trust, and obedience from me, but the very first thing that the yes required was surrender. I had to lay down my path and my plans to follow the instructions and voice of the Holy Spirit. That surrender has included many tears and endings I've had to grieve. Yes, it's included facing fears of not having the provision or financial security I want, but beautifully, it has also included assurance of knowing I am following the voice of God. I can trust that I am exactly where I need to be, and that is what I want most in life. The fact that you're reading this book is proof that God has met this surrender with even more joy, peace, power, and provision! There are many more miracles to come because I said yes to my choice of surrender.

Surrendering To His Will

You might be wondering about the difference between God's instruction and His will. Instructions from God are actions He asks of specific people. God asked me to leave the comforts of my job to finish this book, but He certainly doesn't ask everyone to take that same individual action. God's will, however, comes directly from His Word and His biblical promises. Those truths never change, and we are all called to walk according to that will. I want to share my sweet roommate's story with you: how she used the power of choice to surrender to His will and saw the miraculous manifest in her physical body. Several years ago, Cara was studying the book of 1 John in a Bible Study, and He revealed to her that she was afraid of His love. 1 John is all about the love of God, and as an example of God's love and generosity, her Bible study leaders were led to entrust the group with a certain amount of money. They challenged the group to give that money away. The truth and love that was represented in that act felt overwhelming to Cara, and even caused anxiety over what she should do with the gift. She did diligently give the money away, but struggled and debated on the right place to give this gift throughout the process. This gift to be given away wasn't meant to cause fear, but it did for her. This self-sacrificing love that she read about in 1 John and experienced from the Bible study leaders revealed the fear in her heart. Oftentimes, generous gifts will do that.

Cara felt if she could have earned the gift, she would have felt better about receiving and stewarding it. These feelings of unworthiness and fear caused her to want to build a wall up around her heart so that she would not have to encounter that sacrificial love again. A couple of years after that experience, Cara was at a church worship service and felt the Spirit of God heavily in the room. Cara shared with me that the worship that day was sweet, and it was as if she could feel the love of God surrounding her. As they all worshipped, God kept reminding Cara of His great, self-sacrificing love. That day, the pastor invited those who needed healing to come up and receive prayer. Cara saw others from around the room go up for healing, but while she had a physical need, she knew it would be easy for her to bury or ignore. When Cara was 16 years old, she had pulled her back, and every year or so, it would seize up. She would lay on the floor in agony for up to a week at a time, unable able to sit or stand without her back locking up in pain. The doctor had told her she ruptured a disc in her lower back and that her options were either to have surgery at the age of 22, which would probably lead to further debilitation, or live the rest of her life dealing with the pain until the surgery was unavoidable. That's not what any 22-year-old wants to hear. So, she buried her need for healing and figured she would just have to deal with the suffering for the rest of her life. She told herself it could be worse. Chin up and bear it. She was tough. She could handle it. It's not that Cara didn't want the healing, but she was concerned that maybe her problems and pain weren't worth God's attention. Perhaps you've felt this way too.

But that day during worship, she wondered, "Could the self-sacrificial love of God heal my physical body?" Thank goodness for Jesus and His love! In that holy moment during worship, as people were going up to receive their healing, Jesus asked Cara if she believed He loved her enough to heal her back. He was asking her to surrender– to stop acting like this pain was her burden to bear and she had to handle life alone. He invited her to surrender to His love, and to act on the belief that He loved her enough to notice her pain and cared enough to heal her. Cara's back was totally healed that day because when He called, she chose to surrender her insecurity and instead to trust in Him. God's will for Cara was to walk in and trust His love.

Could a lack of surrender be a reason why you aren't walking in freedom or seeing miracles in your life? Only you and God know that, so take a deep breath. Is your heart pounding in your chest? Is God showing you an area of your life where you need to surrender to Him? What do you need to stop resisting or hand over? What do you need to stop controlling or abandon? I'm grateful for all the therapy, recovery programs, and treatments I've done in my life because they kept me alive, and ultimately God used all of it to bring me into a more authentic and deeper relationship with Him. One thing I do want to say, even with the risk of you being offended and setting this book down, is that I don't believe any freedom or recovery is lasting without a relationship with Jesus. God's will is that we would have a relationship with Him through Jesus. What I've learned in my own journey is that I could only do "recovery" from anything for short seasons, because at some point I would always get discouraged, overwhelmed, and give up. We all stumble, and I'm not talking about perfection, but in myself, I did not have the power to be free from the eating disorder, addictions, and death.

The Product Of Surrender

When all I had was my own strength, I always came back to hopelessness and death, and I wholeheartedly believe the best surrender we can ever make is to give our hearts and lives to Jesus. The more I learn to "open my hands up and give Him control," as the Tenth Avenue North song says, the more miracles I see in my life. The power of your choice to surrender is the beginning of seeing miracles in your life, too. That's the product of surrender: freedom, beauty, joy, miracles, and so much more! Start by asking God to come into your heart. Ask Him to speak to you, show you His nature, and reveal who He is, because the more you know Him and His true character, the more courage you'll have to surrender and give Him the things that are keeping you from your freedom and miracles.

We all have so many things to surrender, and I'm continuing to learn that in each new season it brings more moments of needing to surrender. The good news is that somehow God always turns our moments of surrender into beauty. January 14th, 2015 was my first day walking through the doors of Mercy Multiplied, and what a surrender it was. I gave up normal everyday freedoms; I couldn't use television or social media to numb the pain I was carrying inside. I couldn't call up a friend for support and empathy. I also couldn't hurt myself or run to other destructive behaviors. I didn't know life without destroying and hurting myself, and when I walked through those doors, all I could do was surrender and trust God to make something beautiful. That night, wondering how I'd ever find a way to want to live, God showed me something extremely precious to my soul. He showed me that being at Mercy was going to be one of the hardest things I ever did in my life. I had many demons to face and much to grieve. And yet, in that same moment, He also told me that being at Mercy was going to be one of the greatest gifts I had ever allowed myself to receive.

In Ann Voskamp's book *The Broken Way*, she says, *"Why are we afraid of broken things? Why are we afraid of suffering? What if the abundance of communion is only found there in the brokenness of suffering- because suffering is where God lives? Suffering is where God gives the most healing intimacy."*[13]

What was done to me in my childhood caused suffering that I didn't know how to move past or get rid of. To face and grieve that old suffering was a whole new type of, well, to be honest, suffering. I had to allow myself to feel that old pain I'd run from. Ann also wrote about suffering, *"This is always the choice: pain demands to be felt- or it will demand you feel nothing at all."*[14] It hurt to ignore and push down the anguish from my past, and frankly, it ached even more to turn and address it. Nevertheless, the miracle of surrender is this: when you choose to face it and feel your pain, you can give it to God and let Him do the healing. That was my precious gift and miracle from Mercy.

You've likely noticed by now that lyrics are significant for me. As we conclude the power of choice to surrender, I come back to my favorite lyrics from that All Sons and Daughters song, "Today's surrender is tomorrow's freedom." What I surrendered during those days at Mercy produced a freedom in my life that I never thought possible. Each time I come back to choosing to surrender, to let go of the things weighing me down and abandon myself to trusting fully in Christ, I can experience and walk in deeper freedom. We all have the choice to surrender to His instructions and will, and when we make that choice, it produces healing, freedom, and miracles.

---

13. Ann Voskamp, *The Broken Way: A Daring Path into the Abundant Life*. 2016. Grand Rapids, MI. Zondervan, 34.
14. Ann Voskamp, *The Broken Way: A Daring Path into the Abundant Life*. 2016. Grand Rapids, MI. Zondervan, 28.

Chapter 4

The Power of Choice to Forgive

Forgiveness. This word can feel alarming, and even offensive, when you've been hurt, abused, and beaten down. Yet when you are the one who has caused the hurt, you desperately yearn for this word. It can be hard to forgive others, and just as challenging to forgive ourselves. In our power of choice to forgive, we must decide to:

- Forgive Others
- Forgive Ourselves

In previous seasons, both forgiving and receiving forgiveness have felt unattainable at times. My experiences and conversations with others have taught me I'm not the only person who has felt this way. Let's take a look at both aspects of our choice to forgive in this chapter.

Forgive Others

Before Mercy, I thought I knew what it meant to forgive, but I was missing the richness and depth of this choice. I knew I was *supposed* to forgive. I knew I had been forgiven of so much by God, and yet I was still imprisoned by what had been done to me. I love listening to teachings by Joyce Meyer. She has a very powerful story and has overcome so much in her personal life. A common theme she covers is the importance of forgiveness.

One of the most powerful talks I heard from Joyce was at a 2016 conference in St. Louis. I was deeply moved as she shared how God can heal the soul. She explained that one of the ways healing comes is by completely forgiving everyone who has ever hurt you. I've experienced unforgiveness as a prison, and maybe you have too. My anger towards my parents and the pain they caused me used to consume my mind. I remember that as my mind and heart sizzled with anger, I could feel the burn in the pit of my stomach as well. I don't doubt that anger also contributed to my chronic ulcers.

One of the most powerful things Joyce said at the conference was, "Hatred towards someone doesn't change or impact them, it negatively affects you. Unforgiveness is like drinking poison and expecting the other person to get sick." I carried that weight longer than I ever needed to, and certainly felt its effect on my emotional and physical health. My new Global Senior Pastor at Citipointe Church, Pastor Mark Ramsey, shared similar thoughts with our congregation when he visited this past spring. I heard an amen ring in my heart when he spoke these words, "Forgiveness is not as much about letting them be free as it is keeping our hearts free." Make sure you go back and say that with an Australian accent, as one of my favorite things about my new Pastors is that they are from Australia. I'm learning everything sounds better with an Australian accent, especially great quotes!

When carrying the emotional and physical consequences of unforgiveness and anger became too challenging, my next strategy was to try to convince myself that the pain didn't matter. I believed that if I told myself it didn't hurt, maybe that would become the truth. That was only a short-term defense mechanism as I was eventually faced with the reality that numbing the bad also comes with the cost of numbing the good. I realized that in order to truly forgive those who have hurt me, I had to let myself feel the magnitude of the pain.

One of my favorite men of the Bible is Joseph, the son of Jacob, whose story is recorded in the Old Testament. Since I'm single, friends often ask me what "my type" of guy is, or what kind of man would be the perfect type for me. It sometimes surprises people, but Joseph is at the top of my list. His faith, courage, and perseverance inspire me. I could always use more of that in my life, and I respect men that carry those characteristics. Joseph's story starts with tragedy, loss, and heartache, but through his choices and God's redemptive power, there ends up being purpose from the pain. I encourage you to read his radical story, starting in Genesis 37. Joseph was hurt by his brothers and even people he genuinely helped. If anyone could claim that they had a right to hold onto unforgiveness, Joseph might be first in line. God was faithful with showing Joseph mercy and favor, but humans failed Joseph time and time again. In John Bevere's book, *The Bait of Satan*, he imagines Joseph's possible thoughts:

"It seems that the more I try to do what is right the worse it gets! How could God allow this? Could my brothers steal my promise from God, too? Why hasn't this mighty covenant God intervened on my behalf? Is this how a loving, faithful God cares for His servants? Why me? What have I done to deserve this? I only believed I heard from God." I'm sure he wrestled with these or similar thoughts. He had very limited freedom in his life, but he still had the right to choose his response to all that happened to him. Would he become offended and bitter towards his brothers and eventually

God? Would he give up all hope of the promise's fulfillment, robbing himself of his last incentive to live? [15]

Joseph had the right to choose. He could have decided he wanted to remain angry and bitter towards those who had wronged him. If he had chosen that path, I believe his life and story would have ended much differently. He, too, might have had ulcers from the anger he carried around. I also doubt that God would have used a bitter man to save the lives of his brothers and the nation of Egypt during a famine. If Joseph had chosen the path of unforgiveness, he would have blocked out the miracles God had for his life. Thankfully, that's not the path Joseph chose. Joseph chose to believe that no matter what happened in his life, God was bigger, and God had a plan for his life. I'm sure Joseph had his moments of doubt, but because he believed God could use all things for good, he was able to forgive the people who had wronged him. Joseph proclaimed to his brothers in Genesis 50:20, *"You intended to harm me, but God intended it for good to accomplish what is now being done, the saving of many lives."* (NIV)[16] I don't know what miracle lies on the other side of your forgiveness, but when you align your choice to forgive with God's power, you can unleash freedom and miracles for your life.

When I realized the importance of forgiveness and how it impacts our relationship with God, I knew I had to find a way to let my anger go. I wanted the freedom I heard forgiveness could bring, but I didn't know if I could handle walking it out. I think its human nature to want the benefits without having to work hard or feel pain to get them. I'm still learning to

---

15. John Bevere, *The Bait of Satan: Living Free from the Deadly Trap of Offense*. 2004. Lake Mary, FL. Charisma House, 26.
16. *The Holy Bible, New International Version*, (NIV). 2011. Grand Rapids, MI. Zondervan Publishing House.

trust during moments I don't understand, and although I'll probably never enjoy pain or suffering, I do believe there's a purpose that can be birthed in those moments that we can't get any other way. Tony Sutherland, the author of the book *Grace Works*, came to speak at my church about what it means when God asks us to renew our minds. He shared that one of the ways we renew our mind is by "shedding the past." Tony described carrying the past as carrying a dead man on our backs. Yuck! This compelling image is true when you think about it. Carrying the past is like carrying something that is over and decaying. It doesn't feel good or serve a purpose, and others certainly don't want to be around it. That day Tony was speaking, he brought a greater depth to a verse I have read dozens of times, Mark 11:22-25:

Jesus was matter-of-fact: "Embrace this God-life. Really embrace it, and nothing will be too much for you." This mountain, for instance: Just say, "Go jump in the lake"- no shuffling or shilly-shallying - and it's as good as done. That's why I urge you to pray for absolutely everything, ranging from small to large. Include everything as you embrace this God-life, and you'll get God's everything. And when you assume the posture of prayer, remember that it's not all asking. If you have anything against someone, forgive- only then will your Heavenly Father be inclined to also wipe your slate clean of sin. (The Message)[17]

Tony said that whenever we stand praying, according to that verse, we must forgive any offense or hurt we are carrying. He pointed out the irony that some Christians try

---

17. Eugene Peterson, *The Message, The Bible in Contemporary Language*, (MSG). 2002. Colorado Springs, CO. NavPress

to get mountains to move but skip over the command that they must also forgive. Tony enthusiastically began singing the chorus of a song by 4 Him, "Get Down Mountain." The song passionately proclaims that *mountains need to move out of our way*! Tony made his point that day by expressing that in order to get that mountain to move, that God tells us we need to forgive! As hard as forgiveness can be, it's a major prerequisite for experiencing miracles in your life, just as it was for Joseph. The only way mountains move is by God's power and miracles! Forgiveness is a part of what will release Christ's mountain-moving power.

The scriptures of the New Testament are clear that we need to forgive. One thing that really confused me in my journey of forgiveness was that I would make the choice to forgive, but then that icky feeling would come back up, resurfacing with my hurt and anger all over again. Whenever that feeling returned, I wondered what I was doing wrong, and each time doubted that I had really forgiven. It was a never-ending cycle with all my major hurts. I'd think I had forgiven only to feel the pain of the offenses return. My biggest breakthrough with forgiveness came through a staff member at Mercy Multiplied, Lauren. She taught me that despite popular belief, forgiveness isn't a feeling, it's a choice! This was eye-opening for me.

So, if forgiveness is a choice, what does that mean? It means that when you make the active and intentional choice to forgive, then you can pray and ask God to catch your feelings up to that choice. Lauren said that our part is choosing to forgive, and after that, we can ask God to do what we cannot. I cannot control how I feel, but I do believe that God has the power to align my feelings with my choice to forgive. Often that catch up doesn't happen in an instant. While I think it can, I believe our faith and trust in God grows more when we depend on Him to persevere through challenging emotions. A greater measure of faith is required for perseverance, and a greater measure of faith is grown from it. This process, however long it takes, deepens our relationship with God. Lauren taught me that anytime Satan tries to convince me that I didn't really forgive, I must remind him of the choice I made and continue to ask God to catch my feelings up to that choice. That revelation was a game changer for me and helped me to end the cycle of unforgiveness.

One of the most significant people I chose to forgive was my mom. I now have so much compassion for my mom and the life she lived, but that wasn't always the case. As a teenager, I could only see the ways she had hurt and disappointed me. There were many moments where her drinking and abuse of prescription medications got in the way of loving me well and caused her to miss out on things I wanted her to be there for. She stole money from me to support her habits, and the bank told me the only way to get it back would be to sue my own mother. Sometimes, life looked like wondering if there would be dinner, and even taking the lack of provision as a good thing for my eating disorder. On her worst days, my mother convinced me that my blood family didn't love me anymore because of my faith, and even led them to believe I was the one stealing pain medications. There was so much I was angry and hurt about. All I could see was myself and my pain. I wish my mindset would have changed before she passed away on June 11th, 2006. Once she was gone, all I wanted was to have her back and have a shot at a healthy relationship. We were both broken people looking for something or someone to save us.

For the year and a half after her passing, I walked through all the stages of grief. When I came to the final stage, acceptance, I started seeing her not as the mother who hurt me, but as a mom who loved me as best she knew how. I've heard it said time and time again in the recovery world: hurt people, hurt people, and free people, free people. Yes, my mom was a hurting person who I believe was haunted by her past, and she did unfortunately pass some of her pain onto me, but I can't move on in this chapter without sharing how she loved me the best she could. On many days, her love was wonderful.

My mom loved giving gifts, and I like to believe my love for generosity comes from her. She didn't even need a reason to give. If she saw something and knew it would bring you joy, she'd buy it for you. I remember her reading with me when I was little, and I believe my love for reading is inherited from her. I've been told when she was growing up, she'd lock herself in her room and read for hours. She was also a brilliant photographer, and she captured many moments of our family's lives that would have otherwise been forgotten. Oh, and the beach! The ocean and sand had a way of washing the pain from my mother's eyes and giving her peace. As I grew to see my mother as someone who loved me the best she could, I was able to consider and accept my choice to forgive her. And now, when I think of her and her life, I see love.

Forgive Ourselves

The choice to forgive those who had hurt me, disappointed me, or abused me produced many miracles in my life. I've been able to live more freely, serve more whole heartedly, and love more deeply. There was another layer waiting, though. I didn't have to just forgive others, I also had to learn to forgive myself. That self-judgment piece was even harder for me to address than forgiveness towards others. Like many of you,

I've been my own worst critic, and to be capable of receiving God's love, I had to be willing to let go of my own wrongs and shortcomings so I could pick up God's grace and forgiveness. Earlier in this chapter, I said that to someone that's been hurt, forgiveness can be a scary word. However, to the one who has done the hurting, forgiving yourself can feel almost impossible.

It took a long time for me to learn how to forgive others, and perhaps it won't surprise you that it has taken me even longer to learn how to forgive myself. Can you relate? I found that underneath the unforgiveness and anger towards others were all ten of my fingers pointing back towards me with self-judgement. I've made just as many mistakes, if not more, than the people I've had to forgive. Let's go back for a moment to the relationship with my mom. As I mentioned, before she passed away, the only perspective I was seeing was how she hurt me. But I want to share what happened in the few weeks before her passing. May of that year, I was leaving for my first overseas missions' trip to the Middle East. My mom and I did not see eye to eye on my faith or the fact I was going across the world to talk about my faith, but she was happy for me that I had an opportunity to see the world, something she was not able to do in her lifetime. Although she was deep in her alcoholism by this point, she still made sure I had a video camera to capture my trip and gave me a great big hug as I left. When I arrived safely in the country, the first phone call I wanted to make was to my mom to let her know I had made it to the Middle East. When she didn't answer the phone call, I was quite upset and assumed that she probably didn't answer because she was drinking. I left a sassy (and to be real, very rude) voice message, and decided it was her loss for not answering. I went about my trip in the Middle East and didn't think about it again until two days prior to finding out my mom had passed away.

On that day we had a long bus ride, and I was reading the book *Captivating* by John and Stasi Eldredge. One of the chapters in the book focuses on the relationship challenges between mothers and daughters. While reading that chapter, God gave me a Holy Spirit conviction and told me I needed to apologize to my mom about my attitude towards her. Although I knew God was obviously right, I was stuck in my pride. I felt like the only way I could say "I'm sorry" to her was if she said it to me first. Two days later when I found out she had died, not only was I heartbroken over the loss, but haunted by the fact I'd never get to tell her that I was sorry. And the last thing she heard from me was the sassy voicemail. It took a lot of counseling, grieving, and time with God to be able to release my wrongs from the relationship with my mom. One thing I discovered in my forgiveness journey was that choosing to forgive my mom helped me to show myself grace and learn how to forgive myself.

I know some of you might be thinking, "But Lindsay, you don't know what I did. If you knew what I've done, you'd understand that it's unforgivable." You might be right, but only partially. I don't know what you've done. I may or may not have made the same mistake, but I do understand feeling like things I did were unforgivable. I think Paul, formerly Saul, from the Bible may have felt this way too. Can you imagine being Saul, ravenously killing followers of Jesus and wholeheartedly believe you are doing what's right, only to have your worldview turned upside down? In a moment, Saul was blinded by Jesus' presence and voice, and from then on, he was never the same. He went from murderer of Christians to sold out for Jesus. In 1 Timothy 1:15-16 Paul wrote,

Here is a trustworthy saying that deserves full acceptance: Christ Jesus came into the world to save sinners- of whom I am the worst. But for that very reason I was shown mercy so that in me, the worst of sinners, Christ Jesus might display his immense patience as an example for those who would believe in him and receive eternal life. (NIV)[18]

If Paul, who claimed he was the worst of sinners, could be forgiven, who are we to say Jesus' sacrifice wasn't enough to cover us as well?

The year leading up to me going to Mercy Multiplied was the lowest point of my life for so many reasons, with one primary issue being that I completely hated myself. I couldn't even recognize who I was anymore because my sin had taken me farther than I ever wanted to go. I vividly remember the night when I realized my sin had broken an already hurting man's heart. After an excruciatingly painful conversation saying goodbye to him, I got in my car, opened my sun visor's mirror, and started screaming and sobbing uncontrollably. "I hate you so much, and I just want you to die!" I repeated that awful phrase at myself in the mirror, full of self-loathing. It was at that moment my own struggles with alcohol, cutting, an eating disorder, and promiscuity all came to the surface and I felt completely and utterly unforgivable. I no longer felt worthy of even talking to God or praying. I felt dirty, horrible, shameful. But God didn't leave me in that despair on my journey of learning how to forgive myself.

While I was at Mercy, I had the beautiful gift of being prophesied over by Jane Hamon and Ashley Lackie, from Santa Rosa Beach, Florida. God saw the hatred and unforgiveness I

---

18. *The Holy Bible, New International Version,* (NIV). 2011. Grand Rapids, MI. Zondervan Publishing House.

had towards myself, and He wanted to speak light into that part of my heart through the prophecy. As Jane listened to the leading of the Holy Spirit, she said:

The Lord says, "Daughter, I've been going to the very root of some of the things that set you up for these cycles in your life. The cycles of self-destruction, the cycles where you wanted to opt out of life. The cycles where you covenanted even with death." The Lord says, "Daughter, I've broken the covenant with death. I've broken your covenant with death, and you wondered, 'God, did I go too far to where your grace didn't touch me? Did I go too far with some of those things that I got involved in that I'm outside now of your ability to forgive me?'" And the Lord says, "Daughter, I have forgiven you already." And the Lord says, "Daughter, see, you've been able to choose life for yourself, but you feel guilty because you didn't choose life at one point. I want you to know that I'm cleansing you, I'm healing you, I'm releasing you from judgment. I'm releasing you from the judgment of your own heart that you've carried." The Lord says, "Daughter, do not look back. Don't look back with guilt, don't look back with shame, what was is under the blood. What was has been forgiven. And you know that, except there's a 'yeah, but' in every conversation, and that's because you haven't forgiven yourself. I am delivering you from the grief of those decisions. I'm delivering you from the grief of those things that have hung over your head, and the sorrow, the deep, deep sorrow that you just don't seem able to get free of. You tried every kind of thing to get free of that sorrow and it just doesn't seem to want to loose you. Now, Father, I just thank you, Lord, that from her very root of her being you are rooting up the spirit of grief and sorrow. Lord, you are rooting up every accusation and every blame. Father God, I thank you, Lord, that she has aligned herself with the life that is in Jesus Christ, and because of that, every death-dealing decision is now completely put under the blood of Jesus. It's completely forgiven, completely washed away. Now, Father, we break her free from accusation and grief. We break her free right now in the name of Jesus."

That prophecy was the beginning of accepting that even I, another worst of sinners like Paul, could be forgiven. God had taken my sin to the cross, paid the price, and had truly forgiven me. That day, my faith went from being a concept, knowing God had forgiven me, to a core belief in my heart. Receiving that forgiveness from God empowered me to make the choice to forgive myself.

I also want to introduce you to my sweet friend, Emily. If you know anything about the DISC profile or the Enneagram, Emily is a very high I and a seven, which means she is the most extroverted, outgoing, fun, and genuinely caring person you will ever meet! When I first moved to Nashville, Emily was one of the first friends I made. Emily stands out to me as someone who loves the Lord and loves people very well, and before knowing more about her story, I would have never guessed she struggled with unforgiveness in the past. The Emily I know carries an atmosphere of joy and freedom that follows her wherever she goes. Back in 2010, she found herself in a toxic and unhealthy dating relationship. She didn't recognize it at the time, but because of bullying from her childhood, there were lies that she believed about herself that influenced the way she let men treat her. Emily ended up losing her virginity to this man she was dating, and in this toxic relationship, it turns out that sex was all he wanted.

After that point things changed in their relationship for the worse, and he acted very angrily towards her. Emily, who came from a Christian family, felt that by having sex before marriage she had gone past the point of forgiveness. Satan had convinced her that she had even lost her privilege and right to pray and talk to God. Carrying around the heaviness of shame and guilt she decided to reach out to her sister, Joanna, to tell her what had happened. Joanna loved her sister so well in that moment by telling Emily that she needed to break up with this boyfriend and encouraged her to see a Christian counselor. Emily listened to the advice of her older sister, and while they had been close, it was in that moment Emily and Joanna became best friends. Emily doesn't know where she'd be today without the help of her sister.

Emily's counselor knew there was something under the surface going on because of the anxiety and unforgiveness she was experiencing. It was certainly not okay how Emily was treated by this man, but there was something deeper that was preventing her from accepting God's forgiveness. It was through her time in counseling she was able to process her past bullying and how it impacted the way she let men treat her. It was also where she learned how to forgive herself and the men who had hurt her. Emily shared with me that she will never forget her miracle moment. She was processing her past in counseling and God gave her a picture of His love. In this image she saw the Lord standing in front of her. He didn't say anything to her, but He took the man she had sex with, and the other men from Emily's past who had hurt her and put them over His shoulder. With all those men on His back He nailed Himself to the cross. Through that image, Emily knew God was speaking to her that she was forgiven by Him and that she could forgive herself. Her mindset and perspective changed that day and she learned that no matter what she does or has done, she is never outside of the Lord's graces.

God didn't stop there though; He also gave her another image that allowed her to forgive those who had hurt her. Emily saw herself in her safe place on the beach. All those who had hurt her were represented as sail boats. As she picked up each sailboat and released it into the ocean, God asked her to let them go and be free. God knew what she needed to see in this vision to forgive both herself and others. As she now looks back on her past, she no longer sees the lies that stemmed from the ways she was bullied as a child. She has been able to replace those lies with the truth that she is never alone and is always protected by God. During counseling, Emily saw herself picking up the armor of God that is talked about in Ephesians 6, and instead of being hurt by the bully, she saw the arrows bouncing off her armor. Emily's miracle is that she no longer is affected by the hurt of the past, and her power of choice to forgive opened the door to healing and freedom. Since then, she married a man of God and has precious twins- a boy and a girl! I'm so grateful for my dear friend and the beautiful life she gets to live because she has chosen to align her choices with the power of God by forgiving herself and others.

Once you've grasped the concept of forgiving yourself, it is a breath of fresh air. A deep inhale and exhale. It's a release from judgment and a washing of sweet mercy and grace. All of us have been both the offended and the offender at different times in our life, or maybe even sometimes at the same time. Let's choose to walk out of the prisons of anger and hate, and into the sweet cleansing of receiving and giving grace. Pressing into the power of your choice to forgive both others and yourself will open the heavens to see the miraculous in your life. As Nancy Alcorn, the founder of Mercy, likes to say, "You can't argue with a changed life." God has done it for me, and I know He'll do it for you too.

Chapter 5

The Power of Choice to Have Faith

There's so much to be said about faith. One thing that is clear in scripture is that faith is a requirement of the Christian journey, and a key component of our effectiveness in God's kingdom. Read over these scriptures and see if you can begin to feel something bubbling up inside of you:

Now faith is the assurance of things hoped for, the conviction of things not seen. (Hebrews 11:1, English Standard Version)[19]

For we walk by faith, not by sight. (2 Corinthians 5:7, ESV)[20]

And without faith it is impossible to please him, for whoever draws near to God must believe that he exists and that he rewards those who seek him. (Hebrews 11:6, ESV)[21]

And Jesus answered them, "Have faith in God. Truly, I say to you, whoever says to this mountain, 'Be taken up and thrown into the sea', and does not doubt in his heart, but believes that what he says will come to pass, it will be done for him. Therefore I tell you, whatever you ask in prayer, believe that you

---

19. *The Holy Bible, English Standard Version*, (ESV). 2016. Wheaton, IL. Crossway.
20. *The Holy Bible, English Standard Version*, (ESV). 2016. Wheaton, IL. Crossway.
21. *The Holy Bible, English Standard Version*, (ESV). 2016. Wheaton, IL. Crossway.

have received it, and it will be yours. (Mark 11:22-24 ESV)[22]

...your faith might not rest in the wisdom of men but in the power of God. (1 Corinthians 2:5, ESV)[23]

For in it the righteousness of God is revealed from faith for faith, as it is written, "The righteous shall live by faith." (Romans 1:17, ESV)[24]

Whenever I read scriptures about faith, I want more of it. Did you feel that yearning as you read? I don't think I could ever get "too full" of faith, and to be honest, this is the area I feel the most attacked by the enemy. If he can get his foot in the door and cause us to doubt, the ground we are standing on feels a little bit less secure. There are many things in our lives that feel or may actually be out of our control. But there are many aspects regarding our faith where we do have a variety of choices. There are specific choices we can make that will build our faith and give us a greater ability to believe. These are to:

- Be In God's Word
- Speak And Claim Truth
- Take Faith Risks

Let's take some time to dig into each one of these choices specifically.

---

22. *The Holy Bible, English Standard Version*, (ESV). 2016. Wheaton, IL. Crossway.
23. *The Holy Bible, English Standard Version*, (ESV). 2016. Wheaton, IL. Crossway.
24. *The Holy Bible, English Standard Version*, (ESV). 2016. Wheaton, IL. Crossway.

Be In God's Word

God's word builds our faith and gives us material to encourage us to keep believing, even on the days when we feel overwhelmed. When I am not renewing my mind and spirit in God's word, it's easier for Satan to attack my faith. What ground do we have to stand on if we don't know God's word and truth? I love how the Bible speaks of our relationship with God through parallels to a shepherd and his sheep. There are many ways in which that is significant, and for me personally, I love how the shepherd protects, provides for, and guides the sheep. One scripture that uses the shepherd and sheep relationship is John 10, verses 1-5, in a section titled "The Good Shepherd and His Sheep."

Very truly I tell you Pharisees, anyone who does not enter the sheep pen by the gate, but climbs in by some other way, is a thief and a robber. The one who enters by the gate is the Shepherd of the sheep. The gatekeeper opens the gate for him, and the sheep listen to his voice. He calls his own sheep by name and leads them out. When he has brought out all his own, he goes on ahead of them, and his sheep follow him because they know his voice. But they will never follow a stranger; in fact, they will run away from him because they do not recognize a stranger's voice. John 10:1-5 (NIV)[25]

I believe one of the ways we recognize our Shepherd's voice is by knowing and being in the Word of God. When I am consistently renewing my mind with the Word of God, it increases my faith. I am empowered to not only recognize

---

25. *The Holy Bible, New International Version,* (NIV). 2011. Grand Rapids, MI. Zondervan Publishing House.

God's voice, truth, and leading in my life, but also to open the door for miracles. The reverse is true as well. When I'm feeling off-kilter or shaky in my relationship with God, I can almost always look back and see that I've not been spending as much private time with God in the Word. *"So then faith cometh by hearing, and hearing by the word of God."* (Romans 10:17 KJV) [26]

A simple way I enjoy being in the Word is teaching it to children. In the Bible God talks about a "childlike faith." When is the last time you've been around a 4 or 5-year-old? You don't have to share my love for being around children, but I dare you to spend a few hours with a child and see how their faith can inspire yours. I love serving at my church, Citipointe Nashville, and a few Sundays a month you will find me teaching the kids five and under. My favorite times with them are worship and Bible stories. Little Jeremiah has taught me that I have no idea how to help potty train a boy to use the bathroom (a process that is hilariously mysterious to me), and his two-year-old little heart for the Lord is breathtaking. He answers my Sunday questions passionately with responses like "God can!" and "JESUS!" Please be sure to add an enthusiastic two-year-old's volume to those quotes. Jeremiah was also curious, inquisitive, and excited to hear about the story of the paralyzed man in Mark 2, who was brought to Jesus by his friends. They cut a hole in the roof just to get him before Jesus, and by faith that man was healed! That man and his friends certainly used their power of choice to have faith and to get him to the presence of Jesus for a miracle. Jeremiah's childlike faith stirred in me a profound hope in God during that moment.

My daily time with God reading the Bible is essential for

---

26. *The Holy Bible, King James Version*, (KJV). 2013. Nashville, TN. Christian Art Publishers.

me to walk in faith. I am convinced this is true for everyone, because we can only stay encouraged for a short time before needing to be filled with more of His truth. Many people I've talked to struggle with making a consistent time to spend in God's word, and it used to be one of my biggest challenges as well. There are so many deadlines, responsibilities, commitments, and distractions constantly surrounding us. It can feel unrealistic to set aside moments for reading. Even when we do plan time to study the Word, there can be occasions where what we are reading feels complicated or perplexing.

My suggestion would be to start simple. If your struggle is finding time, commit to 5 minutes. My breakthrough to having daily time in the Bible started in my car. I found it impossible to concentrate if I tried reading before getting ready for work, and by the end of the day I felt too exhausted to extract anything from the Bible. So, I started simple by getting to work 10 to 15 minutes early to study in my car. It may not sound like much, but it worked! Those quiet moments expanded my faith, and now being in the Bible is a routine for me. This habit extraordinarily blesses me with an overflow of joy, strength, and peace.

If your current challenge is understanding and receiving from the word, pick up a daily devotional or study guide. A few of my favorites are: *Trusting God Day by Day* by Joyce Meyer, *Grace for the Moment* by Max Lucado, and if you like discovering the meaning of words, check out *Sparkling Gems from the Greek* by Rick Renner. The more you spend with God in the Word, the more truth and strength you'll gain. Be in the Word. Let it build your faith. Watch for the miracles that are produced by God's power and your choice to have faith.

Speak And Claim Truth

Speaking truth is one of the most powerful choices I've experienced that has both helped me find freedom and keeps me walking in it today. I used to believe I had no choices in what I thought or how I felt. One thing I want to share for context is that I was born prematurely and when I was only a day old, I had to have emergency surgery to survive. Due to this circumstance, I came to believe a lie that I was born broken, that God didn't create me to survive. I thought I had no choice but to live in depression and anxiety forever. There are many different causes for depression, anxiety, and other mental health issues. I don't believe I chose to struggle with my mental health, and I think most people don't choose to have these problems. However, I do believe that what we choose to say, think, and do can either help us overcome depression or sink deeper into it. I didn't always believe that I could affect my own thoughts, which is why my life used to be so dark and hopeless. It was at Mercy Multiplied that I learned I had a choice.

One of the first things my counselor had me do at Mercy was to write down the negative beliefs I thought about myself, which I would now call the lies I was believing. After I identified the messages I was telling myself, she asked me to seek out the truth about myself and God by praying and reading the Bible. I knew God said I was loved and that He would never leave or forsake me, but my heart didn't really believe that. I could read these truths, but somehow, I couldn't get them to sink down into my heart. Even though I didn't think it would work, I wrote down the truth I *wanted* to believe on brightly colored index cards. Can you picture that huge, vibrant stack?

My counselor told me that I needed to speak those truths

out loud, every day. It felt extremely silly to sit around once a day and speak those words off the cards. At first, I would rush through them just so that I could check the box stating I had done my assignment for the day. When I realized speeding through my cards wasn't the point, I started to put more effort into really meaning those words. Some days, it felt incredibly painful to speak those truths. I desperately wanted to believe those truths, but because I couldn't see them in myself, it ached as I forced the words out of my mouth. I had no idea how speaking was going to change anything, but even on the painful days, I had to trust the process and keep speaking.

I don't want to give pain any attention or glory, but before Mercy I had been sexually abused as a child, was raised by alcoholics, neglected, watched my family fall apart, kept family secrets, cut myself to numb or to feel anything at all, starved myself, watched my dad leave and my parents' divorce, was raped and sexually assaulted several times in adulthood, lost my mom at the early age of 20, drank until I passed out, felt chained to many addictions, put myself in dangerous situations, carried many mental health diagnoses, and tried to kill myself. It felt like an impossible laundry list of things to be free from. Even out of all the horrible things that I did or were done to me, the most painful thing I walked through was living every day wanting to die. It was excruciating, and my mind lived in almost-constant torment. Though I'd begun putting real effort into speaking truth, I had no idea how that choice was going to heal any of the torment. Jami, a staff member at Mercy that helped crack my heart wide open, would even speak the truth out loud some days with me, though she never did it *for* me. She helped me keep this habit even when my mind was trapped in torment. She continued to encourage me that it wasn't enough to try and change a thought with another thought; that I had to speak something different out loud to change that thought.

Then, it happened: something changed. My miracle broke through the web of lies I'd believed. I was walking around the parking lot having spoken those statements by faith every day for six months. I spoke the truth, "I see God healing and transforming my life." My jaw dropped, and I had a moment of holy awe because I realized I could finally see what I'd been speaking daily for six months. I was actually seeing God healing and transforming my life! I'd said the truth, and it had become my reality. God used my choice to speak those truths to radically set me free from the depression, anxiety, and suicide, completely transforming my mind and life. I had a choice to stop speaking the harsh and negative realities of what I felt or saw and to start speaking God's truth and words!

God is still teaching me is what it looks like to hold space for authenticity and faith in my words. He's showing me how to be genuine when I'm feeling down or circumstances are hard, but also continue to speak truth and what I want to see in my life. If I speak anxiety, I see anxiety and I feel anxious. If I speak life, I see life, and I feel alive. Let me be clear, though. One phrase I dislike to the core of my being is "fake it until you make it." Yuck. It gives me a burning feeling in my stomach and reminds me of my dark childhood. Because of all the sin, alcoholism, and abuse that was going on in the home, I had to "fake it" all the time. I know now that my parents were only acting out of their own hurt, but we were expected to keep the darkness a secret and act as if we were perfect. So to me, fake it until you make it means act like things are perfect and I'm perfect. It feels like an invitation to cover up the issue so no one can see it. I never want to go back there. That's what made me sick and run to death. If I don't want to fake it, but I have a choice to speak truth, what does that look like when things are really hard?

I've asked God why I feel so strongly the need to be authentic. He has lovingly shown me that's what He has created me to be: authentic. No wonder it feels like such a sweet word to my soul; that's who and how He created me to be. Authenticity is not an excuse to just speak negatively, but a freedom to share my heart and vulnerability. That is beauty to me. To be genuine, in hope. As God has been teaching me to speak with authenticity and truth, He has brought me to scripture. The Psalms are my favorite examples of this:

"Even though I walk through the darkest valley, I will fear no evil, for you are with me; your rod and your staff, they comfort me." Psalm 23:4 (ESV)[27]

"I love the LORD, for he heard my voice; he heard my cry for mercy. Because he turned his ear to me, I will call on him as long as I live." Psalm 116:1-2 (NIV)[28]

"My comfort in suffering is this: Your promise preserves my life." Psalm 119:50 (NIV)[29]

It seems to me that the authors of these chapters are speaking authentically, acknowledging that pain and suffering exists, but they are not living in that. In the same breath that they recognize hurt, they're choosing to speak of God's goodness and comfort.

Lamentations is another example of authenticity and truth. Chapter 3 starts with saying:

---

27. *The Holy Bible, English Standard Version*, (ESV). 2016. Wheaton, IL. Crossway.
28. *The Holy Bible, New International Version*, (NIV). 2011. Grand Rapids, MI. Zondervan Publishing House.
29. *The Holy Bible, New International Version*, (NIV). 2011. Grand Rapids, MI. Zondervan Publishing House.

I am the man who has seen affliction by the rod of the LORD's wrath. He has driven me away and made me walk in darkness rather than light; indeed, he has turned his hand against me again and again, all day long. (Verses 1-3, NIV)[30]

Sounds like a heavy reality! The passage grows darker and heavier if you continue to read. But when we get to verse 21, something starts to change:

Yet this I call to mind and therefore I have hope: Because of the LORD's great love we are not consumed, for his compassions never fail. They are new every morning; great is your faithfulness. I say to myself, "The Lord is my portion; therefore I will wait for him." (Verses 21-24, NIV)[31]

The English Standard Version ends verse 24 with *"therefore I will hope in him."*[32] As I walk out my life in the authentic way He has created me, it must always include His truth as my reality and hope. I've been diagnosed with an autoimmune disease, but God is my healer, so I walk in hope. I've had seasons of stress when I wondered how God was going to move, and I had to choose to say in that same breath, "I know He will bring peace and freedom." Speaking truth is a choice, hence helping yourself to believe truth is a choice. In times I'm really struggling to believe, I ask God to help me with my unbelief. One of my favorite encounters in the Bible comes from the man who brought his possessed son to Jesus. As he explained the seriousness of his son's situation, he told Jesus,

---

30. *The Holy Bible, New International Version*, (NIV). 2011. Grand Rapids, MI. Zondervan Publishing House.
31. *The Holy Bible, New International Version*, (NIV). 2011. Grand Rapids, MI. Zondervan Publishing House.
32. *The Holy Bible, English Standard Version*, (ESV). 2016. Wheaton, IL. Crossway.

"But if you can do anything, take pity on us and help us." "If you can?" said Jesus. "Everything is possible for the one who believes." Immediately the boy's father exclaimed, "I do believe; help me overcome my unbelief!" (Mark 9:22b-24, NIV)[33]

This man was willing to speak that he believed, and asked Jesus to help him with the unbelief he was experiencing.

As a reminder, *"So then faith comes by hearing, and hearing by the word of God."*[34] (Romans 10:17 NKJV) Speak and hear yourself say the word of God and be honest with God about any unbelief in your heart. He already knows, and by doing these things, you will set your mind free. In Annie Downs' devotional, *100 Days to Brave*, she writes, *"Believing truth is always a choice. In every situation, in every conversation, and in every moment that you begin to criticize yourself, you have the choice to fight for truth or give into the lies."*[35] Fight the enemy and the lies by choosing to speak truth. Speaking it will help you change what you see and believe and allow you to live a life of freedom! If you'd like ideas on truth you can be speaking and claiming over your life, you can find examples in the resources section of this book.

Take Faith Risks

"Faith risks" is a phrase God gave me. Once, He uttered that phrase to bring me into a deeper trust in Him. Has God ever asked you to do something so big that the only way it

---

33. *The Holy Bible, New International Version,* (NIV). 2011. Grand Rapids, MI. Zondervan Publishing House.
34. *The Holy Bible, New King James Version,* (NKJV). 2018. Nashville, TN. Thomas Nelson.
35. Annie Downs, *100 Days to Brave: Devotions for Unlocking your most Courageous Self.* 2017. Grand Rapids, MI. Zondervan, 17.

can succeed is if His favor and provision miraculously show up? That's a faith risk. To be clear, a faith risk is not a foolish action, an excuse for poor planning, or a lack of wisdom. It is a pure faith, driven by a conviction and resolve that God has asked you to do something far beyond what you could ever do by yourself.

The first time God used that phrase with me was when I decided to move to Nashville. Yes, people move to Nashville every day, which is evident by the constantly increasing Nashville traffic. I love Nashville and it has become my home, but beware of getting stuck in rush hour! When I first arrived at Mercy Multiplied, my plan was to move back to Florida at the end if I found the hope and strength to live. It never once crossed my mind that I would go anywhere else. While I was at Mercy, there was another woman in the program that was from Nashville. As God began to heal my heart and give me a hope for my future, I started to have this pull towards Nashville as she spoke about her hometown. I didn't understand that "pull" at first, but when I recognized that God was using that to show me He was calling me to Nashville, I was afraid. I knew moving to Nashville meant change, uncertainty, and telling my family I wasn't coming home. I kept thinking, "Who goes to a recovery program and then moves somewhere they know nobody, have no connections or community, no place to live, and no job prospects?" That made absolutely no sense to me! I couldn't understand how that could be a good thing. I would have never advised someone in my situation to do that, and it sounded like a recipe for disaster and relapse. However, as God continued to speak to me and show me that Nashville was where He was calling me to move, it became a strong conviction in my heart. I knew I had to choose to obey Him in that faith risk.

While I was grateful that He clearly showed me I was to move to Nashville, it didn't mean that process was easy. It was quite a challenging process. You have no idea how many tears the Mercy staff members had to sit through as I worked through the details of the move. To be honest, I think they probably questioned why I would move to Nashville and how God was going to make it real. My faith grew during this time and by the time I graduated from the program, Liz, a staff member who helped me with the planning of the transition and move, told me that it grew her faith to watch God work out the details and unfold His plan. It was clear to her that only His provision and favor that made the move possible. It was also only by His goodness and power that such a beautiful and redeemed life is possible. Nashville was a great faith risk that even those closest to me questioned, but because I took that risk, my faith and God's power produced a miraculous result and life.

There are many faith risks recorded in the Bible. Remember the paralytic man and his friends that little 2-year-old Jeremiah was so curious about? They, too, had to take a faith risk to see a miracle. What amazes me is that yes, that man was healed, but as I dig more into the story I also believe that a greater measure of faith was produced in their lives. Increased faith is another miracle in itself! Every time I step into a faith risk, I see tangible miracles, and I also see a greater measure of faith produced in my life. I also love the story of Abraham in Genesis. He left all he knew to go to a place that was unfamiliar. I'm sure I experienced some of what he did as I moved to Nashville. God has showed me that I am to have a faith like Abraham's; one willing to go and do whatever He asks of me. By following, I'll experience His favor and blessings.

I want to focus on two more men from the Bible and how

their choices impacted their lives: King Saul and the then-teenager, David. We all face both big and small choices, and how we make our choices tell us a lot about who we are. I've heard it said that faith is defined by being able to live in the tension when what we see and what God has revealed to us don't line up. When reading about the lives of King Saul and David, it becomes clear that one chose to avoid a faith risk while the other chose to step into it. Picture King Saul and young David on the battlefield facing the biggest giant they have ever seen, Goliath. This giant was taunting, cursing, and threatening God and His people. Destruction and hopelessness enveloped the land. There was no one who could possibly overcome such a strong and vicious warrior. As Israel's king, it was supposed to be Saul's job to fight Goliath, but he sought solace in hiding and shrinking away from the risk. David, however, chose to jump into the faith risk. While he was yet a boy, a leader only over sheep, he put his faith in the God who called him to be king. He took this faith risk even though he could not see any evidence of God's promise in his life yet. I believe that his faith risk produced the miracle of saving God's people, and I'm sure it also strengthened and encouraged David's faith in his future.

The Israelites' escape out of Egypt was another massive faith risk. Read the book of Exodus to follow this adventure. The Israelites wanted freedom from captivity, but slavery was also all that generation had ever known. I can put myself in their shoes and imagine the questions. "How do we know what we are going to will be better?" "What if we anger Pharaoh, what will happen to us?" "How will we survive the journey?" "How will we be provided for?" Perhaps they even asked what I often find myself wondering: "Am I strong enough for this risk?" In the midst of all the fears and unknowns for God's people, they had to make the choice to put their faith in God. In what looked like their final despair, they were enclosed by the fiercely pursuing Egyptians on one side and an uncrossable sea on the other. They needed a miracle to survive. God asked Moses to take a faith risk, and that risk brought them out of captivity and saved their lives. This story that can still increase our faith today. My friend Ryan, who you'll be hearing more about his family in future chapters, pointed out to me that in this story there are only three things we need to focus on to see the miraculous:

1. <u>Fear Not.</u> Believe that God is with you in the risk He is asking you to take.
2. <u>Be Still</u>. Quiet your heart and look to God, instead of trying to perform for Him or people.
3. <u>See the Salvation of the Lord</u>. He alone will perform the impossible.

As scary as faith risks might look and feel, when God is calling you to take that risk, don't shrink away. If you do, you'll miss out on seeing the miracles He will produce out of the chance and steps you take.

I've been reading through the Old Testament since returning home from Israel, and several times a week I'm finding myself in awe of how God is speaking to me. I used to avoid the Old Testament because it felt too challenging to read. I enjoyed hearing teachings on the Old Testament, but I found it too hard to read for myself, struggling to pay attention through all the lineages and laws. Having now seen and experienced Israel, I find myself wanting more and more of the Old Testament! What stands out to me most in this season is how God reveals Himself to Moses as the I AM. It is in Exodus 3 that Moses sees the burning bush and God declares that He is the I AM, revealing that the I AM is sending Moses as a deliverer. Exodus 3:14 says, *"God said to Moses, 'I AM WHO I AM. This is what you are to say to the Israelites: I AM has sent me to you.'"* (NIV)[36]

As I continue to read in the Old Testament about the Israelites wandering through the wilderness and preparing to enter the promised land, God continues to remind them that the same I AM who was with them as they exited Egypt is the same I AM that is with them in the wilderness. He is the same I AM that goes before them into the promised land. The Israelites go through their ups and downs, but as they time and time again call on the name of the Lord by faith, they continue to see the I AM performing miracles in their midst. God is so consistent at reminding the frazzled Israelites that He is the same I AM that delivered them from Egypt. He knew they were forgetful people, prone to be swayed by the world and their circumstances. Today, we aren't so different. As we take faith risks and see freedom and miracles take place in our lives, allow this story from our Christian heritage to encourage us that the very same I AM that performed those miracles is the same I AM that will continue to empower us to believe for the impossible. He, the I AM, is faithful.

I pray this chapter created a longing in your heart: that you would desire and choose to have more and more faith. I never want to reach a point in my life where I feel like I have enough faith. In each season when I've chosen to believe and risk, not only has God increased and built up my faith, but He's also combined that faith with His power. In this process, I have seen the impossible and miraculous. Thank you, Jesus, for this life and for freedom. I encourage you to ask God how you can choose to have faith, wherever you are in life.

---

36. *The Holy Bible, New International Version,* (NIV). 2011. Grand Rapids, MI. Zondervan Publishing House.

Chapter 6

The Power of Choice to Press In

    There are many moments in our lives where we area given the opportunity to draw close to God. The choices I've made to "press in" developed an increased intimacy with Him. It's similar to the friendships I have formed here in Nashville. I had to spend time with these friends to get to know them, but the closeness didn't form until I pressed into those relationships. Closeness is developed by genuine trust. What do I mean? Well, there's a difference between sharing activities like watching movies and playing games verses allowing someone to witness our pain, sorrow, or fear. Madeleine, one of my favorite people, became a good friend by spending time with me and introducing me to one of my favorite games, Pandemic! Spending time together was good, but there was another level waiting. Once I opened up my heart to her and allowed her to be amid the hard circumstances I was going through, she became one of my very best friends.

    It can perplex people when I say this, but my most special moments with my friends are when they are vulnerable enough to cry in front of me. It's certainly not because I enjoy seeing my friends cry or want them to be sad or in pain. It's because I don't take their tears lightly. I know for someone to be willing to cry in front of me, there has to be a level of intimacy and trust between us. Pressing into our relationship with God is like that; it requires intimacy and trust. Our choice to "press in" brings us one step deeper or further with God. Pressing in means not being satisfied with anything less than all He has for us. We want to be fully immersed in this relationship.

A few ways that we can develop that intimacy with God is by using our choice to press in through:

- Prayer
- Experiencing God's Presence
- Learning To Hear The Voice of God

By making an effort to press in, the closeness that is grown in our relationship with God creates an atmosphere to encounter the miraculous all around us.

Prayer

Prayer used to intimidate me. Before I understood it as an intimate conversation and connection to God, it felt like a performance. What were the right words to use? How long should the prayer be? Is God mad at me if I repeat things? Yes, that last question was a legitimate fear of mine. I remember being told as a child that God would get mad at me if I repeated requests in the same prayer. It's strange how one small false belief can be passed down and become a major fear! I started to enjoy and understand prayer when I began keeping a prayer journal. Writing down my prayers not only kept me from getting distracted, but it also served as a record of His faithfulness when I would reflect and see how He had answered different prayers. There are so many ways to talk to God: prayer journal, praying out loud (by yourself or with others), silent prayers being lifted to God, and even asking others to also bring your request to the Lord. What that means is when we pray, we are making an active choice to press into our relationship with God. Prayer is a powerful and intimate connection to God, and as we see God move in our lives, it builds our faith and hope for what we don't yet see; those things we are trusting God for in our lives.

This past Christmas, I was so excited to go back and visit my family in Florida, but as I was making plans for the visit, my original travel arrangements fell through. Here I was, only 6 weeks before Christmas, needing to buy $700 plane tickets (yikes)! That was more than I had saved. I was disappointed, as I felt strongly that I needed to be with my family for the holidays. In that moment, I knew I had to trust God for a solution and the provision. I said a prayer to God, and I also knew I needed to reach out to a friend in the midst of my discouragement. I asked my dear Pandemic-playing friend, Madeleine, to pray for the situation. While I didn't know how God would answer, I had to press into Him and trust that He'd provide a way for me to get to Florida, or that He'd provide me with peace if I couldn't go. I had to cling to this promise: *And whatever you ask in prayer, you will receive, if you have faith.* (Matthew 21:22, ESV)[37]

Not even five minutes later, another dear friend, Oksana, texted me and told me that she felt led to get me home for the holidays. She wanted to give me the cash needed that I was lacking for the flight. That, and a special gift from my Grandmother, got me all the way home to Florida. I was in awe that God would place that generosity on Oksana's heart, and it no doubt increased mine and Madeleine's faith. What a fun text to be able to send to Madeleine– the report that God had met my seemingly large need in only five minutes!

---

37. *The Holy Bible, English Standard Version*, (ESV). 2016. Wheaton, IL. Crossway.

Prayer, at least for me, isn't usually answered that quickly, or in the ways I expect it to be answered, but it has produced such a harvest of faith, intimacy, and a deepening of my relationship with God. This is especially true when I take the time to reflect and see how His hand has been at work in my life. Prayer grows my trust in God, even when I don't get the answer I wanted or expected. Faith doesn't always come in the exact moment of disappointment, but as I continue to surrender and press in, it will get stronger. I still don't have the husband or children I'm praying for, but I won't stop praying.

I can keep asking and trusting because I've seen other jaw-dropping answers to prayer. I've seen friendships restored. I've seen lives redeemed. I've seen miraculous provision. I've seen prophecy and words of knowledge in action. So, I know I can trust Him with my future. Those other answered prayers have built my belief for this one to be answered too. Even when I was in the darkest season of my life and felt I didn't deserve to pray, I couldn't help but plead with God that He would get me through the doors of Mercy Multiplied. I knew if that was all I prayed and He got me there, then there was potential for a miracle. Don't ever give up praying and communicating with God, because that choice to pray will fuel the impossible and the miraculous in your life.

Experiencing God's Presence

As I write this section on God's presence, I think it's my favorite because of the peace I feel when I'm experiencing His presence. There's nothing better. There are an unlimited amount of ways that you can press into God's presence and experience intimacy. The choices are endless. An encounter with God doesn't have to look a certain way, and I'll share some ways I've chosen to press in through my own experiences.

Even if your "way" isn't presented in this chapter, please know that God uses many ways and situations to draw us into His presence.

Perhaps you're struggling to find the ways you experience God's presence, or feel disconnected from Him. My advice is to look for things that make your heart come alive. I feel most alive and at peace in nature, in intimate times of prayer, and during corporate worship. I also experience God's presence when I am crafting and creating things. Around babies or children, I can feel God strongly. That may make you smile or laugh, or you may not relate as you think of the chaos, stress, or responsibility associated with kids. While I know it can sometimes be tough, very little can put me at peace more quickly than when I see a child smile. What brings you life, peace, and joy? Those are ways to experience God's presence in your daily life.

Just last night, I was babysitting for my good friends Ryan and Madeline, the friend who prayed with me for my Christmas plane ticket. Their sweet boys are Judah Ryan and Noah Brave, and I've gladly accepted a role as "auntie" in their lives. Judah was not happy to be put to sleep by someone other than his parents, but to be able to comfort him in a moment of sadness helped me to experience the heart of God. I love how he was clinging to me and allowing me to comfort him in his tears. As for Noah, his smile could melt an army. He's just starting to baby giggle and show affection. It's incredible to me how God knit him together in Madeleine's womb, and already knows that little boy's destiny and purpose. Not only is it incredible that God has plans for their lives already at such a young age, but being around them also reminds me of how my heavenly Father loves, comforts, and tends to me. There's no better expression of God as my Father than nurturing the little children God has placed in my own life. For me, these moments with the boys feel like basking in God's presence.

I once heard a pastor explain the presence of God physically feeling "velvety" inside the body. That might not make sense to you if you've never tangibly felt or experienced God's presence, and maybe it doesn't feel that way for everyone, but I do understand and feel that at times when I'm in God's presence. The only way I can think to explain it is that it feels like my heart is tingling, and that God Himself is tenderly massaging my heart. It may sound like an odd description, but when I'm in those moments it's so powerful and peaceful that I never want to leave. During prayer and worship these are holy moments to me.

Before attending Mercy Multiplied, one of my most memorable experiences in God's presence was after leaving a toxic and sinful relationship. I felt used, manipulated, hurt, and extremely shameful that this relationship took me further from God than I ever wanted to go. I even wondered if I had run so far from God that I couldn't be forgiven for getting involved in this forbidden relationship. I was desperate for God to take me back, but I felt unworthy to enter into His presence.

Although I wanted to stay hidden because of my shame, a mentor of mine invited me to a new church service she had recently attended. At that service, she experienced a touch from God and knew that getting me in His presence would help me encounter His love and forgiveness. Her invitation gave me a choice to stay isolated at home or to press in to experience God's presence. I'm so glad I chose the latter. I arrived at the next service broken and afraid, but greatly longing to return to His heart. The pastor that night asked those who wanted a tangible touch from God to come to the altar and lift their hands to the Heavens. He came and prayed for each person wanting to receive this touch. I knew I wanted and needed that touch. What I was given from God's presence that night was so powerful that I couldn't even hear a word the pastor prayed for me, I fell to the ground and only felt peace and a washing in God's grace. God's manifest presence during that service cleansed me from my sin and removed the chains of shame. In some cases God frees us by the daily decisions and choices we make, and then there are moments like this one where getting in His presence breaks everything that is not of Him in an instant.

I believe God's presence is one of the most effective ways to break shame. When we press in, shame cannot survive the glory and fullness of who God is. I had another impactful encounter with God when the shame of what had been done to me as a child did not want to release me. I said all the prayers and broke all the soul ties, but I felt this shame clinging to my chest. It felt like it was a thick black tar substance clinging to my spirit and nothing I was doing loosened its grip. As I continued to pray and surrender this shame to God, my counselor at Mercy played the song "How Can It Be," by Lauren Daigle. As the song played, the presence and Spirit of God began to melt away the shame, and by the time the song ended it was gone. I was free. It was a miracle; God used the song and His presence to do something I could not accomplish on my own.

Press into the presence of God. It does more than just break shame– His presence heals sickness, brings truth to our lives, frees minds, gives peace, and even shows us His divine direction. Again, I encourage you to look for the times and places when you feel alive, at peace, passionate, and purposeful. Take note of the moments when you're left awestruck by His glory and goodness. Once you've identified those moments and places, keep choosing them. God wants you to experience Him in ways that are unique to you. Setting yourself up to be in those situations is choosing to press into God's presence.

Learning to Hear the Voice of God

Another way to press in is learning to hear the voice of God. Some Christians have heard the audible voice of God. While I (and most others) haven't heard Him audibly, I've learned to hear Him in other ways. If you get away from the distractions and noise and ask Him to speak, He will.

It was in May of 2015 that I really started to hear the voice of God. Going into Mercy, I had major trust issues, and that didn't just change when I walked through their doors. Even after being at Mercy for months, I was still trying to figure out if people were really rooting for me. At the beginning of May, I was convinced I could only trust myself and God. I felt God give me permission for a week to trust Him alone. Perhaps I was a bit rebellious in turning my heart away from trusting others, but I believe God used that week to teach me and prepare me to hear from Him. The next week, the night before my appointment with my counselor Katie, God spoke to my heart. He said, "I've allowed you to trust only in Me this last week, but tomorrow Katie is going to ask you to do something, and I need you to trust her." As scary as trust was, I knew I had to obey what God had spoken.

I wasn't prepared to do what Katie asked of me that next day, but since God had told me I needed to trust her, I did. Katie gave me the assignment of not talking to anyone for a whole week! 7 days. No talking. 168 hours. 10,080 minutes. 604,800 seconds. That's a lot of silence! I could not believe that after a week of me essentially closing others out, I'd have to take another week of isolation and loneliness that I thought would come from not being able to communicate. Contrary to my expectations, something incredible started to happen.

Katie had been teaching me how to hear the voice of God, so she encouraged me to take that week to press in, and to listen and communicate more directly with Him instead of communicating with others. Since that week, I've continued to hear some pretty incredible things from the Lord, but that week remains one of my sweetest times with Him.

He taught me in that week how to listen to Him and ask Him what He wanted me to eat, so that I didn't need to be controlled any longer by the eating disorder. He spoke to the deadly perfectionism, telling me He never expected me to be perfect in order to be worthy of His love. I began to sit on the front porch at the Mercy home and experience what I call "front porch peace." I'd bring my journal and pen and sit and talk to God as the sun was setting. I'd start by thanking Him for those moments, and then write down questions my heart longed to ask Him. As I sat there and sought Him with my whole heart, He spoke. He'd tell me what to write in response to my questions. That time, learning to hear from Him, was precious to my soul. It can be hard to still myself on busy, crazy, or stressful days, but it's always worth it when I do. His voice brings freedom.

I've heard my friends Madeleine and Ryan share their story many times as they meet new people, and it never gets old. Their journey and relationship have been a testimony of God's eternal love and faithfulness! Like all couples, Madeleine and Ryan needed to hear from God and be willing to obey His voice if they were going to have a God-honoring relationship that lasted. During their engagement, things had become so challenging in their relationship that they wondered if they were truly supposed to be together. Because of some of the dysfunction and lows they were experiencing, they decided to take two weeks apart from one another. No texting, no calling, no seeing each other. They both knew they needed dedicated time to allow space to hear from God. What a brave choice to make for a couple in crisis! During those two weeks, Madeleine felt attacked by the enemy. She was anxious and having panic attacks, which made it feel almost impossible to hear from God. Madeleine told me she knew that the only way she would be able to hear from God was if she resisted her fears and put her "spiritual pants" on to fight the attacks.

In this spiritual battle, God revealed to Madeleine that her fears stemmed from control issues and a lack of trust. He showed her that the only way to be free was to decide to trust God with her whole heart, and to trust Ryan as her potential future husband. For her, it took many small steps to release the fear and control. On the last day of those two weeks, Madeleine finally experienced freedom and breakthrough. She got to a point of intimacy and trusting the Lord so deeply that she only wanted to marry Ryan if God gave the word. She knew it would hurt like hell if God said no, but she decided she would trust God if He said no, and she would trust God if He said yes. She wanted to be in His will more than anything else she desired, and she'd committed to press into hearing his voice. Madeleine also needed a shift to happen in the area of her identity. If she continued to get purpose and identity from Ryan, they would have been a crutch for each other. That type of relationship typically leads to disappointment, division, and strife. Madeleine heard from God during this time that her identity and security were in Him, not in Ryan, and that revelation from God changed her heart.

Madeleine decided she needed to pray a specific prayer to hear from God on whether she was supposed to marry Ryan. As she prayed, she asked God that if His answer was to marry Ryan, then Ryan would say to her, "Madeleine, you are a part of my calling." What a bold prayer to pray– I can only imagine how much faith that required! Madeleine believed that she would hear from God and that He would confirm His will, and she was also speaking words of faith that He would confirm it. Two days after Madeleine prayed that bold prayer, Ryan called and asked her to meet him at their pastor's house. In those same two weeks, Ryan was also believing that he would hear from God on his relationship with Madeleine and if they were to be married.

Ryan had gotten to the point in their relationship that he was afraid of not being with her, but he was also fearful of getting married to her because of their struggles. Lists of pros and cons were not creating clarity. Ryan knew he had to press in and hear an unshakable word from God. God had already been teaching him that if he learned to hear His voice in the small things, then he'd be able to hear Him in the big things. There had been random little things God asked of Ryan. One day God told Ryan he needed to call his sister, and another day God simply asked him not to have coffee. Ryan found that as he obeyed in those small things, his heart became softer and more sensitive to hearing God's voice. He was learning that we can't only listen to God on some subjects; we need to be willing to listen and obey in all aspects of our lives. At the end of those two weeks, God spoke to Ryan and revealed He wanted them to get married if Madeleine was willing to be the woman God talks about in 1 Peter 3. Ryan believed he was hearing God correctly, but he was also concerned about what he heard because he didn't have a lot of repetition yet of hearing God's voice in the big things. He asked God for a confirmation, just to be sure.

It reminds me of Gideon in the book of Judges. He also humbly asked God a few times for confirmation to make sure he was hearing God's voice correctly. With confirmation from the Lord, Gideon became willing and confident to follow the voice of God. An hour after Ryan prayed for confirmation, his pastor called and asked him to come over. When Ryan arrived, his pastor said to him, "God told me that the Lord had already given you the answer you needed and that you wanted a confirmation." That word and confirmation through his pastor was the push Ryan needed to call Madeleine and ask her to come over that night.

This is where their stories of hearing from the Lord collide. Before meeting that night, Ryan asked Madeleine to also read 1 Peter 3, and she told him she wanted to be that woman the scripture talks about. Before any other reason, her motivation was that God wanted her to be that woman. After that, Ryan told her, "God told me I am called to be with you and marry you." This is the part of the story that makes my eyes well up with tears! Madeleine said that answer to prayer was the only word she needed to marry Ryan. The way God spoke to her in that moment built up her faith and her trust in both God and Ryan. Ryan also said that, in this moment, his trust put him in the right position to hear God's voice and confirmation. This decision to press into God through hearing His voice strengthened both of their relationships with Him. I'm so grateful for my friendship with this amazing couple, and I love that God so cares about us and the specifics of our lives that He will speak to us and confirm His word. He always does this when we take the time and space needed to hear from Him. I believe that both our ability to hear from God and the results we see in our lives because of listening are miracles!

It takes faith to make the choice to press in and not be content with the status quo, and it's through those pressing in moments that we deepen the intimacy we experience with God! Choose to press in through prayer, experiencing God's presence, and hearing His voice. You'll be amazed at the power of that choice as you come to know God more.

Chapter 7

The Power of Choice to Worship

When you read the word worship, what do you think of? What do you picture? My mind automatically thinks of church, and I see myself singing and praising God with my arms lifted high. My heart seems to soar during corporate worship. There is something about coming together and singing songs of praise that brings me closer to the heart of God. Choosing to worship is a powerful choice we have, and another avenue that can usher in God's miracles. Worship, however, does not have to look one way. While I can share so much about singing and gathering, I also want to look at our acts of service and our giving as forms of worship too. If we are to google the definition of worship, it brings up:

1. *The feeling or expression of reverence and adoration for a deity*
2. *The acts of rites that make up a formal expression of reverence for a deity*
3. *To treat someone or something with reverence and adoration*[38]

I believe this entire definition is about expressing our love

---
38. Worship. 2019. In *Merriam-Webster.com*. Retrieved July 24, 2019, from https://www.merriam-webster.com/dictionary/worship.

and devotion towards God. As we give God the reverence and glory He is due, something changes in our lives and connects us with the spiritual realm. Ways we can choose to worship include:

- Corporate Worship Services
- Serving
- Tithing And Giving

Corporate Worship Services

Let's start by looking at corporate worship. Have you seen or heard stories of people being healed during worship at church or revival meetings? I believe that happens not only because God's presence brings miracles, but our active choice to worship and praise Him does too! There have been and will be times in my life where singing and worshipping Him does not come naturally or easily. As much as I love singing and letting myself be expressive during worship, there have been times where I didn't want to sing, and times where it was emotionally or physically painful to do so. One of the most painful times for me to worship was the season after my mom passed away.

My beautiful mom had her own hurts and demons she had to face in her life, and it saddens me that I never got to see what my mom's freedom could look like. Our relationship with one another was filled with a lot of brokenness, pain, and darkness. When I was in high school, there were times when I'd stay home from school and we'd lay in bed together, watching Lifetime movies in a dimly lit room. Words didn't have to be spoken. When they were, we mostly didn't get along, but we both understood that life felt dark and broken.

I was aware of her battles with prescription drug abuse and alcoholism, and I knew it was severe, but I never thought I'd lose her the way we did.

When I moved away to college, I was still struggling with most of the negative behaviors and coping mechanisms I grew up with, but I was also beginning to grow in my faith and learn more about God. I was so excited when I learned I could go on mission trips to tell others about God and the faith I had in Him. I spent several weeks that summer in the Middle East doing just that. I loved the culture and how warm the people were. I had never met more relational people in my life! We were served tea everywhere we went, treated like family even though we were just meeting these people, and were given the best of all food and treats. Halfway through that trip, we took a few days off to rest, recharge, and have some fun in the country. One day everyone else on my team was enjoying swimming in the hotel pool and having fun, but I couldn't let myself participate. I had a certain heaviness on my heart, and I couldn't help but feel I had somehow failed my sister and my mom. My whole physical body and emotions ached from that heaviness I felt. I spent the day in bed crying, praying, and journaling. I didn't know in that moment what I was experiencing, but I now know that my soul was experiencing separation and loss.

That next morning, I knew something was very wrong. Six months prior, I started having a few different versions of a nightmare where I was sitting with two women while I was on the phone with my dad, who told me that my sister found my mom dead. While I believe those nightmares were not from God, I do believe He chose to use them to help prepare me for the grief. That's why when my roommate at the hotel called me out of the shower because two female leaders were coming to talk with me, I knew it had to be about my mom. Still, I prayed that I was simply in trouble, or that I did something wrong and needed to be scolded. I knew that wasn't true, but I wanted it to be. When those two women, Erica and Sarah, came to my room, they handed me a phone and told me I needed to call my dad. My devastated dad softly revealed that my mom had passed away the day before, and that my sister had been the one who found her. I instantly put my head in Sarah's lap and started sobbing. The hardest I've ever cried was in those moments after finding out she was gone. My body had experienced her being taken away that day before, and the confirmation of her death felt like more than I could bear. That next week was a complete blur as I tried to get home from overseas.

    I was so confused. I pleaded with God in that season. Until that point, the most painful, gut-wrenching, life-altering experience I had been through was rape. This happened not only as a child, but also as a teenager shortly after graduating from high school. As horrific as that was, I told God I'd rather be raped every day if that meant having my mom back. That was the only depth of pain that I knew how to relate it to. I had no idea how to carry this new type of grief and anguish. I didn't understand why she had to die. How could God be good and sovereign if He knew she was headed toward death and still let it happen before she found freedom in Him? She had passed away from a heart attack caused by a prescription drug overdose. It was preventable. I went through all the phases of grief: denial, anger, depression, bargaining, and finally acceptance. Before making it to acceptance, I argued with God through each phase.

    I share this story about the loss of my mom because not only did it shake my faith and relationship with God, it significantly impacted my ability and desire to worship. How could I sing about God being good when I really didn't know if that was true anymore? How could I sing about His glory and power when He couldn't even save my mom? I think we've all been through a loss like that, perhaps a family member, mentor, friend, spouse, or even a child. I believe the death of a loved one feels so unbearable to our soul because God didn't create us for death. He created us to experience abundant and eternal life, and it's only through the fall of man we've had to face death's sting. It hurts so badly because we were never meant to experience it.

If you have lost someone or are facing that possibility, I highly recommend the book *A Grace Disguised* by Jerry Sittser. In his book, he shares his own personal story of losing multiple family members in a horrific car accident. Throughout his journey of healing, he discovered how the soul grows and is impacted by loss and the grieving process. As I read the book, it felt like Jerry knew exactly where I was in the course of grief. He discusses how our soul expands to hold more loss, agony, and ache than it's ever felt before when someone close to us has died. Grief's heaviness and depression come from our soul stretching to carry more pain than it's ever felt before. I was certainly feeling and carrying that ache. As I mentioned, it even took away my desire to worship. I felt I'd be a hypocrite and a fraud if I sang those worship songs and lifted my hands when I didn't know if I believed it anymore. Choosing to worship seemed fake and disingenuous to me.

Jerry's concept of the soul growing doesn't stop with just a deeper capacity to carry pain, thank God. He goes on to share that because our soul grows its capacity for loss, that means that our capacity has also grown to carry a deeper and larger amount of joy.[39] Worship, the very thing I'd been avoiding,

---

39. Jerry Sittser, *A Grace Disguised: How the Soul Grows Through Loss*. 2004. Grand Rapids, MI. Zondervan.

was eventually the way I experienced that newfound depth and space for joy. The winter after my mother died, I was at a Christian conference with the college ministry I was a part of called CRU. As much as it felt inauthentic and painful to worship, I was encouraged by Sarah, one of the women who was with me when I found out my mom had passed, to worship God for who the Bible says He is, and not for the pain and emotions I was experiencing. I trusted Sarah, so I decided to press into that thought. That night, during worship, I chose to sing and lift my hands to God even though it was not what I felt. Because of that choice, He provided an incredible miracle. As I was worshipping, I physically felt God reach down and touch my heart and tell me that He was giving my joy back. That choice to worship brought the miracle I needed to start healing from my mother's death. It allowed me to start trusting and growing in my relationship with God again, even experiencing this deeper capacity and fullness of joy.

It's easy to sing and worship when times are good, and it's probably the most impactful to our faith when times are hard, and we have to actively choose to worship. That's probably also when we feel the need the most for a miracle in our lives. When my heart is aching, my favorite go to worship song is "Even When It Hurts (Praise Song)" by Hillsong UNITED and "Surrounded (Fight My Battles)" sung by Michael W. Smith. If you're hurting and worship is the last thing you want to do, I encourage you to create a playlist of songs that are meaningful to you. This curated list will allow God to meet you where you are. Our worship doesn't need to look perfect and pretty, and in fact it can be full of tears. It just needs realness and authenticity before God, choosing to reach up to Him for who the Bible and the truth says He is, no matter what our emotions or circumstances claim.

My roommate Cara, who experienced the physical healing in her back, has seen God do many incredible things in her life through her passionate worship. Living with her, I see her heart for worship. While it looks like it comes naturally for her, it is an attitude she had to make choices to press into and develop. She still has to actively choose to worship on the hard days in order to see the miracles. Growing up, Cara had participated in more worship sets than you could ever imagine. Her parents were missionaries, and that meant her family was at their local church services every time the doors were open– no matter what continent they were on. Even though Cara had been worshipping her whole life, she admitted that she didn't always know what true worship was. It wasn't until after she was fired from her first nursing job that she experienced a true desperation for God. She went on a holy rampage trying to find answers to her situation. Through friends, God led Cara to a godly woman and her Bible study. This woman invited Cara to her place of worship. Because of this woman's joy and freedom, Cara looked forward to this service with great expectations. While Cara was anticipating blessings from this service, she still carried burdens of shame, confusion, doubt, insecurity, fear, and strife. There was a battle for her heart and mind that day, which made it challenging to enter into worship with God.

One moment she was standing, hands raised in awe of God, and then the next sitting with her head in her hands, wondering what she was doing there. She wondered, "God, can you even hear me? Do you even want to listen to me?" Then she stood up again, trying to mentally work her way into His good graces, only to be undone with the knowledge that she couldn't be perfect. It took hours for the truth to sink in: that she had to choose to worship. She had to choose to lay aside herself and her inadequacies. She had to choose to lay aside every burden and every thought that was trying to set itself up against the true knowledge of Christ. She had to choose to think on His goodness, His grace, and the truth of His Word as she acknowledged that He alone was worth her attention. No more distractions were welcome. As a very simple song played, Terry Clark's "We've Come to Worship You," the Spirit of God began moving. Cara saw miracles unfolding: healing in people's bodies, minds being set free, and individuals receiving the Holy Spirit. In the midst of all the miracles surrounding her, her only focus was worship, and Jesus sought her out.

As she stood at the front of the room, truly worshipping for maybe the first time in her life, her pastor asked her, "What do you want from the Lord?" She said she had absolutely no words. If you know Cara, that statement alone is a big deal! In the chaos of her mind and the agony of those few seconds, she could not utter one sentence, much less the desire of her heart. In her choice to worship she had just seen a breakthrough, but she was still was so burdened by her own insecurity and confusion that she couldn't even speak. God had taken notice of Cara's struggle and spoke to a man of God who was there. He said to Cara, "The devil's been hounding you, distracting you. You have been chasing your tail like a dog. But tonight, you will be set free." That man then told Cara to place her hand over her heart and the elders of the church prayed for her. The Spirit of God then miraculously moved in her life.

It's hard to explain when the power of God meets our earthly bodies. It is the most renewing sensation, but the powerful presence is too much for our flesh to sustain. In that moment of prayer, Cara fell to the ground, feeling such a sense of peace. The burdens and weight had been lifted. The newness of life pulsed through her. She was sobbing, but they were sobs of release as she surrendered to this peace. One of the elders held out his hand and helped her back to her feet as they finished worshipping. As it became time for the pastor to share the word, he asked Cara to share what happened that day in worship. The answer was simple: peace had come. The miraculous power of God set Cara free from strife, confusion, and chaos that night. It was because she made the choice to worship.

I love what scripture has to say about how we should sing and worship:

"Come, let us sing for joy to the LORD; let us shout aloud to the rock of our salvation." (Psalm 95:1, NIV)[40]

"My lips will shout of joy when I sing praise to you- I whom you have delivered." (Psalm 71:23, NIV)[41]

"Go ahead and give God thanks for all the glorious things he has done! Go ahead and worship him! Tell everyone about his wonders! Let's sing his praises! Sing, and put all of his miracles to music! Shine and make your joyful boast in him, you lovers of God. Let's be happy and keep rejoicing no matter what. Seek more of his strength! Seek more of him! Let's always be seeking the light of his face. Don't you ever forget his miracles and marvels..." (Psalm 105:1-5a, TPT)[42]

---

40. *The Holy Bible, New International Version,* (NIV). 2011. Grand Rapids, MI. Zondervan Publishing House.
41. *The Holy Bible, New International Version,* (NIV). 2011. Grand Rapids, MI. Zondervan Publishing House.
42. *The New Testament with Psalms, Proverbs, and Song of Songs, The Passion Translation,* (TPT). 2017. Savage, MN. BroadStreet Publishing Group, LLC.

As we use our choice to worship, we see miracles in our lives. We also worship in light of the miracles God has performed in our lives, and this then creates even more joy, gratitude, and miracles.

Serving

Another choice we have regarding worship is our choice to serve. This can be seen in serving one another in our relationships, and with our choice to be involved in serving at churches or other ministries and organizations. I first recognized the benefits of serving while I was a resident at Mercy Multiplied. We had a few serving opportunities, and I had no idea what a positive impact they would have on my life. I believe serving is an act of worship. It is something God has called His church to do, and as we serve and worship in this way, it gives God the glory He is due. This verse applies to how we use our bodies as worship, and I believe serving falls under that: *"Therefore, I urge you, brothers and sisters, in view of God's mercy, to offer your bodies as a living sacrifice, holy and pleasing to God-this is your true and proper worship."* (Romans 12:1, NIV)[43] How we serve and give can, and should be, worship to God.

One of the serving opportunities I had at Mercy was with Joyce Meyer Ministries as we packed up books and supplies to be given to women in jail. It took no official talents or gifts to be able to serve in this way. All I had to do was put the books and items in a bag. While it took no skill, it was incredibly rewarding. I found myself feeling good that I had something to contribute, even in my broken and hurting state. As I packed each individual bag, I was able to say a silent prayer

---

43. *The Holy Bible, New International Version,* (NIV). 2011. Grand Rapids, MI. Zondervan Publishing House.

for each woman that would receive them. Pastor Jillian, from Citipointe Church in Nashville, pointed out what I had learned from serving. Pastor Jill said in a sermon "We serve and give thinking we'll be the blessing but discover we are so much more blessed to give than receive!" I love that. We impact and bless others when we serve, but God somehow created this process so that we receive an even greater blessing.

One chapter in Lisa Harper's book, *The Sacrament of Happy*, focuses on how the sacrament of happiness can change the world through compassion and serving. In this chapter, Lisa even compiles scientific evidence to prove what these qualities produce in our lives. This list includes a decrease in stress hormones, increases in wellbeing and productivity, and greater feelings of fulfillment. It doesn't matter how we serve, only that we do.[44] I see the benefits when I choose to serve as an act of worship. I know that learning how to serve at Mercy impacted the healing, freedom, and miracles I experienced there, beginning with the lesson that I had value and could contribute something as "little" as packing up gifts to bless other women.

I will never forget when Jami, a staff member at Mercy, shared her personal story with us. She talked about some of the hardships and struggles she'd faced in her life, and I think most of us could relate to aspects of the path she had walked. The part of her story that impacted me the most is when she said, "Serving saved my life." In the midst of her own personal battles, she had begun to reach out to help and bless others. As she served, God was able to not only meet her needs, but also healed and redeemed her story. She also saw a shift in her perspective. What greater miracle could you ask for than to be able to say, "Serving saved my life" and mean it?

---

44. Lisa Harper, *The Sacrament of Happy: What a Smiling God Brings to a Wounded World.* 2017. Nashville, TN. B&H Publishing Group, 149.

What I'm about to share is hard to write, but necessary. God has nudged me to respectfully speak on this, and I trust that God will use it to encourage you to serve even when it feels hard. I don't currently have a relationship with my father. I love him and I have forgiven him for things of the past, but until he can forgive himself and be freed, it's not healthy for me to be in communication with him. I knew breaking communication was going to be extremely hard and painful, and I dreaded it for several months before I followed through with it. The last Father's Day before we stopped speaking, I woke up exhausted and sad, wanting to ignore the fact it was Father's Day. It felt too painful knowing I didn't have the type of relationship with my dad that I wanted. I was scheduled to serve with the two-year old children that morning at church, but nothing in me wanted to get out of bed and face the world. I even (incorrectly) felt I deserved to stay in bed because of the pain of my relationship with my own father. However, the commitment I'd made to serve that day got me out of bed, knowing they were expecting my presence. God always shows up when we make a sacrificial choice to worship, and the sweetest miracle happened that day.

Four darling girls rushed me as I walked through the door. Sweet little Kennedy, Abigail, Destiny, and Skylar asked me, in their two-year-old little words, to sit with them, read them books, to hold them. They even played with my hair. That day the Lord ministered to me more through those toddlers than I ever could have given back through serving. In a sense, serving redeemed that day, but I had to make the choice to get out of bed and show up to serve in order to receive that blessing. Your choice to serve, wherever and whatever that may be, will give you a positive and renewed mindset as you are helping. Serving will pour out blessings and miracles in your life.

Tithing And Giving

The final area I want to touch on as an act of worship is our tithes and offerings to God. I had always heard we were supposed to give God ten percent of our income back to Him, but it took me a long time to understand the reasons and the spiritual implications. Outside of pure obedience to a biblical command, I wasn't sure what the impact was. I began faithfully tithing while I was at Mercy. I started learning about tithing while I was there, and even though I had little to give, I'm grateful the habit and obedience of giving financially started. Giving financially never came easily to me in the past because I had so many fears about money. As silly as it may sound, I still sometimes fight fears about not being provided for and ending up homeless. Financial fear is an area Satan tries to rattle if I'm battling a season of insecurity. However, since my time at Mercy, I've made the choice to faithfully give each month, and I've always had all my financial needs met. That's not a coincidence! When we worship with our giving, it is a seed being sown. I know it will bless where it's being used, and it will open the doors for breakthroughs and miracles in my own life as well.

I love hearing Pastor Jillian preach on tithing. She has encouraged me with Biblical truth and the spiritual effects we experience when we tithe. When she taught from Malachi, she explained the covenant promises we received when we tithe. My top three takeaways from that sermon were:

1. It honors God when we tithe as an act of worship
2. We are sowing into something bigger than us when we tithe
3. We can claim God's provision and protection when we tithe

Now that I know more about tithing and have experienced blessings from it, I love the concept of sowing and reaping. I think it's incredible that we can sow something as small as a seed and receive an entire harvest. I know because I give faithfully, the door has been opened for miracles and the impossible in my life.

When I moved to Nashville, I had some bad luck with cars! The enemy intended these problems to create stress, frustration, and hopelessness. I did have my moments of panic, but as I kept pointing myself back to God and continued to tithe, He showed up! To give you the short version: I unexpectedly had to buy two new to me cars in a six-month time frame. At the time, I worked at Ramsey Solutions and was following the Dave Ramsey plan, so going into debt for a new vehicle was not an option. I had been saving, but not enough to purchase a new car. In the process of needing those cars, God provided me with rental cars and great friends to cover any gaps during renting. When it came time to purchase the first car, God provided ALL the cash needed to purchase it, and when I had to buy yet another car unexpectedly, He provided all the cash needed for that one too! When all was said and done, He provided $25,000 in a nine-month time frame! It was through an increase of income, gifts, insurance money, selling car parts, and more. Now, it wasn't all fun and games– I had to ask for help getting to work or borrowing cars, and I had to be faithful in God's timing. I truly believe because I faithfully tithed through all that mess and trusted God to provide, He showed up with miracles!

If you have any questions about tithing, I encourage you to study what the Bible says about it and asked a trusted pastor or leader. As Malachi 3:10 says:

> *"Bring the whole tithe into the storehouse, that there may be food in my house. Test me in this," says the Lord Almighty, "and see if I will not throw open the floodgates of heaven and pour out so much blessings that there will not be room enough to store it." (NIV)*[45]

I want that kind of blessing pouring into my life. And, in the famous words of Dave Ramsey during the weekly staff meetings I was a part of, "We are blessed so that we can be a blessing." It builds my faith to see how God miraculously provides for all my needs, and as I give, He continues to bless me and others through it.

I hope you're amazed at how many ways we can worship God, offering Him our love and adoration. Whether it's corporate worship, serving, giving, or something completely different, I encourage you to ask God today how to worship Him in the season you're in. No choice to worship is small in His eyes. Your ongoing choice of worship opens the doors for a lifetime of freedom.

---

45. *The Holy Bible, New International Version,* (NIV). 2011. Grand Rapids, MI. Zondervan Publishing House.

Chapter 8

The Power of Choice to Be Thankful

Practicing thankfulness and gratitude may sound simple, but seeing the strength, peace, and joy that have overflowed from this choice in my own life, I know its value. Because I spent my life in a victim mentality prior to Mercy Multiplied, I felt I had little to be thankful for. When I started to practice all the prior choices and saw God at work in my midst, it was then that I recognized His goodness and realized my need to cultivate a heart full of gratitude. The choice to be thankful includes several decisions:

- Intentionally Reminding Ourselves To Be Grateful
- Removing Obstacles That Block Gratitude
- Thanking God Even When We Feel We Shouldn't Be Grateful

Intentionally Reminding Ourselves To Be Grateful

Expressing gratitude and thankfulness is a command in the Bible. It's not just God fishing for compliments, but another means for us to connect with Him. Let's examine two scriptural passages on thankfulness:

"Shout for joy to the LORD, all the earth. Worship the LORD with gladness; come before him with joyful songs. Know that the LORD is God. It is he who made us, and we are his; we are his people, the sheep of his pasture. Enter his gates with thanksgiving and his courts with praise; give thanks to him and praise his name. For the LORD is good and his love endures forever; his faithfulness continues through all generations." (Psalm 100: 1-5, NIV)[46]

"Let the message of Christ dwell among you richly as you teach and admonish one another with all wisdom through psalms, hymns, and songs from the spirit, singing to God with gratitude in your hearts. And whatever you do, whether in word or deed, do it all in the name of the Lord Jesus, giving thanks to God the Father through him." (Colossians 3:16-17, NIV)[47]

This command alone has the power to change our negative mindsets, unlocking wonder and freedom. Because I was extremely depressed and suicidal, I was used to making lists in the past of why I should want to live. I knew there were things I should feel grateful for, but it never seemed to be enough to make me want to go on. Personally, I wasn't practicing gratitude in those moments, just making lists. I don't know exactly how or when that transformation took place to be truly grateful, but I do know that it started small, yet grew like wildfire once the gratitude took root in my heart.

In the darkest parts of my journey with depression and suicide, it felt hard to be joyful or grateful about anything.

---

46. *The Holy Bible, New International Version,* (NIV). 2011. Grand Rapids, MI. Zondervan Publishing House.
47. *The Holy Bible, New International Version,* (NIV). 2011. Grand Rapids, MI. Zondervan Publishing House.

As horrible as it sounds, some days I couldn't think of a single item for which I was thankful. Despite feeling it was impossible some days, I made an active decision at Mercy to look for a few things I did love and enjoy. One thing I've always loved are birds. I love how free they appear, that they always seem to have a song to sing. God talks in scripture about how He provides for the sparrows, and that we should not worry about our own life or provisions, as we are much more valuable to Him than birds. (Matthew 6:26)[48] Because of my love for birds, I decided one day that any time I saw a bird, that was a sign from God, specifically reminding me of how much He loves me. God knows how much I delight in birds, so why wouldn't He want to use those moments to shower me with His love? That may sound silly or simple to you, and yet it has produced more comfort and gratitude than any other single choice.

I wish I could share with you every moment that my heart has burst with gratitude because of the reminder of His love through birds. One day, I was sitting in the Whole Foods parking lot and crying after a hard counseling session. I had no idea how God would give me the strength to get in and out of the store. As I sat there, tears streaming down my face, I looked to the left outside my car. To my delight, there were about a dozen little sparrows hopping and playing near some bushes. My heart leapt with gratitude from the reminder of my Savior's love. Another time I woke up exhausted and downtrodden, but I got out of bed and looked out my window to see dozens of birds sitting in a nearby tree. What about the beautiful hummingbird that visited my apartment porch up on the third floor? A quote on gratitude that I was deeply impacted by from Lisa Harper's *The Sacrament of Happy* is:

---

48. *The Holy Bible, New International Version*, (NIV). 2011. Grand Rapids, MI. Zondervan Publishing House, my paraphrase.

Frisking our thoughts and changing our position can do wonders when it comes to rocking us out of mental and emotional ruts and getting us back on the highway of happy. We really can use our minds to turn our frowns upside down. However, cultivating happiness- that is tending and fertilizing our God-given joy so as to make it grow bigger and bloom more often- requires intentional gratitude. And deliberate thankfulness...delivers a double blessing because gratitude is both the fertilizer and the fruit of happiness. Gratitude leads us towards happiness and it flows from happiness. (Page 131)[49]

Amen! Even as I'm writing this, I'm intentionally noticing and cultivating gratitude for birds chirping outside, even though it is a chilly 27 degrees. Choose to remind yourself to be grateful!

Removing Obstacles That Block Gratitude

If gratitude is a choice that produces miracles in our lives, I can also look back and see how complaining, the opposite of gratitude, keeps us from seeing freedom and wonders. I never intended on being a negative Nancy. In fact, from my viewpoint, I always called it "being a realist." You know those people, or you relate because you are one. For much of my life, I wasn't a glass half full type of girl. As I mentioned, before finding freedom through Mercy, I lived with a victim mindset. Because I believed I had no choice in any area of my life, I felt like a slave to negativity, darkness, and depression. When something went wrong or hurt, it was natural for me to complain about it. I hated when people confronted me

---

49. Lisa Harper, *The Sacrament of Happy: What a Smiling God Brings to a Wounded World.* 2017. Nashville, TN. B&H Publishing Group, 131.

about my mindset, because I didn't believe they could ever understand the pain of what I had been through or what was done to me.

Surely if they did understand, then they'd know it wasn't my fault I felt and acted the way I did. Even with the perspective I have now, I would never say depression was mine or anyone else's fault. However, I do see how complaining, negativity, and the victim mentality can prevent and block us from experiencing freedom, joy, and miracles in our lives. As I continue reading through the Old Testament, I'm tempted to laugh at the silly Israelites and how easily they turn away from God. God is so good, though, at giving me a little tap on the shoulder to remind me again and again that we are not much different from them. I was reading in Exodus 16 about how after one month from when they left Egypt, they were complaining about not having food to eat. Let's pick up in Exodus 16:1-3,

> *Then the whole community of Israel set out from Elim and journeyed into the wilderness of Sin, between Elim and Mount Sinai. They arrived there on the fifteenth day of the second month, one month after leaving the land of Egypt. There, too, the whole community of Israel complained about Moses and Aaron. "If only the LORD had killed us back in Egypt," they moaned. "There we sat around pots filled with meat and ate all the bread we wanted. But now you have brought us into this wilderness to starve us all to death." (NIV)*[50]

As I read the book of Exodus, God used this chapter and the entire book to show me an insight on complaining. The "oh

---
50. *The Holy Bible, New International Version*, (NIV). 2011. Grand Rapids, MI. Zondervan Publishing House.

snap" moment for me was when God showed me that when we focus on complaining, we lose sight of what He has saved us from. These Israelite people were miraculously rescued by God from a horrible existence of abuse and slavery, and just one month later they are saying it would have been better to stay and die in Egypt. Say what? How forgetful! They are basically saying that it was better, or easier to live a horrible existence with food than to trust God to provide them with something to eat in the desert. Needing food in a wilderness is certainly hard, but aren't they following the same God that parted the sea and swallowed up an entire army? Unfortunately, we aren't that different from them, and I'd be a fool to claim with certainty that I would have acted differently.

To me, the point is that when the Israelites looked at their lack of food instead of the God who saved them, they began to complain and lose sight of the miracles God is capable of. The complaining became an obstacle to gratitude. Food is nothing compared to parting an entire sea! It's crazy to think that everything they'd seen wasn't enough for them to keep the faith. I don't think it's because they were bad people, it's because we are all finite and needy for a miraculous God. I wish my time at Mercy was enough for me to never doubt again. Just like everyone else, I still have hard days, but reminding myself of what He has saved me from keeps His goodness in front of me. My season there was one of the most miraculous times in my life, and actively reminding myself of it keeps me grateful, with a heart full of worship and praise for God. I believe God brings us from faith to faith and glory to glory because we need Him to continue showing up as faithful in our lives.

When I complain, I lose sight of what God has done in my life, and in turn, I lose faith in what He can do now. I'll also miss my next miracle if I give up during the in-between season. When I set aside my complaining and focus again on God's goodness in my life, I won't miss out on the miraculous things He wants to continue doing. When the Israelites complained about their lack of food, God still showed up with a miraculous provision, but as you continue reading in Exodus, you discover their pattern was to continue to complain and turn away from God. That pattern cost their generation the miracle they needed most: crossing into the promised land. When you are tempted to complain, I encourage you to give that pain or doubt to God. Let me be clear: don't allow yourself to speak to God with a closed and hard heart of contempt. Give it to Him, and then remind yourself of God's goodness and the ways He has shown up already in your life. This type of gratitude, when life feels hard, will open doors of freedom that no man can shut!

Maybe for you that choice needs to start with something small too. Do you love nature? Colors? Sports? A certain song? I encourage you to start identifying a few things you love and take joy in. God created you and knew you even in your mother's womb, so I believe that our passions and what we take joy in are purposeful; He delights in giving us reminders of His love and showing us those gifts. As I made those "small" choices to be grateful, it has grown into a life of gratitude.

Thanking God Even When We Feel We Shouldn't Be Grateful

You might be asking yourself, "What about the hard things, like flat tires or breakups? Should I be thanking God for those?" I can look back on obstacles from the past and thank God for them now because I see how God has used them for good. I would not be the free soul I am today without experiencing some of those hard moments and trusting God to make beauty from ashes. Perhaps you're wondering about the hard thing that is happening right now, or the piece of your life that is broken and shattered? I wish I could tell you I have all the answers. While I don't have all the answers, I do know that thanking God for the hard things, in the moment, is something He has been teaching me over this last year. I'm a Two on the Enneagram (The Helper), and I feel my Two-ness all the way down to my core. Some days I wish I could masquerade as another personality, but I relate so strongly to the motivation and behaviors of a Two. Pride is something Twos can struggle with, and when I first shared my own struggles with pride to others, it was confusing to friends and coworkers. I'm not that "better than everyone else" type of person. Ian Morgan Cron and Suzanne Stable explain the pride of a Two in this way:

> *Pride is the deadly sin of a Two, which sounds nonsensical because Twos appear to be more selfless than self-inflated. But pride lingers in the shadows of Two's hearts. It reveals itself in the way they focus their attention and energy on meeting the needs of others while at the same time giving the impression they have no needs of their own. The sin of pride comes into play the way Twos believe other people are more needy than they are and that they alone know best what others require...What lies beneath that pride? Terror. Twos fear that acknowledging their wants will end in humiliation and that directly asking someone to fulfill their needs will lead to rejection... It would only confirm what I've known all along: I'm unworthy of love.*[51]

---

51. Ian Morgan Cron and Suzanne Stabile, *The Road Back to You: An Enneagram Journey to Self-Discovery.* 2016. Downers Grove, IL. InterVarsity Press, 115-116.

My pride is not about proclaiming my superiority, it's about being terrified I'm not enough. When I'm not operating out of God's love for me, I try to combat that "not enough-ness" with being as helpful as I can. On healthy days, nurturing and serving fuel my soul. On stressful or challenging days, helping is fueled by trying to earn my worth. I don't have a natural drive to want to be the best, but I do have an underlying fear of being the worst that can paralyze me. If I begin to feel insufficient, my anxieties increase and my self-worth plummets.

The first time I grasped the concept of thanking God for the hard things, even in the tough moment, was about a job promotion I didn't receive last year. Days before hearing that news, I was reading a book called, *The 4 Wills of God* by Dr. Emerson Eggerichs. God knew that getting that book into my hands was crucial to help me walk through this situation. I knew I wasn't getting promoted before I was told because I could see that I wasn't quite ready. I knew that, and not getting promoted wasn't the piece that was hard for me. The part that devastated me was that everyone else in my role was getting promoted. They all were "enough," except for me.

Again, I don't need to be the best, and I wish I could have just been happy for everyone else. However, feeling like I was the worst at my role pulled out every insecurity, every fear, and every word of self-judgment. I wondered how on earth I was going to make it through the moment when everyone else realized that I was the only one not promoted. This felt so closely tied to my worth that I was certainly not wanting to thank God for that circumstance. As I was reading Dr. Eggerich's book and bracing for this situation, I read his words about thanking God in all circumstances, even the hard, bad, and evil ones.[52]   Dr. Eggerich shared several stories that impacted my ability to thank God, even when it felt like I shouldn't be grateful. I chose to thank God for being the only person to not be promoted because that meant I had another opportunity to trust Him. In the moment they made the team announcements, I thanked God with all I had in me and kept moving forward. I didn't receive instant peace, but in each moment that it felt hard and I made the choice to give thanks, it became easier with time.

Now I'm finished with that hard season, and while I don't fully understand its purpose, I know God used it in my life. I'm continuing to find my worth more and more each day in God and not in my abilities, strengths, and talents– or lack of them! It was during this season that God met my hurt, humiliated heart and said, "My daughter, you may be in last place in others' eyes, but in my eyes, you're first." There's no better validation than the words of my Heavenly Father. Giving thanks in a hard situation was an act of choosing to trust and worship God, even though the situation didn't feel good. That choice has allowed God to bring me into a deeper freedom from striving, perfectionism, and performance. He's not finished with me yet in this area, but I'm freer than I was a year ago, and with how strongly this pride used to be embedded in me, I count it a miracle!

One last story I want to share about giving thanks in pain that resulted in the miraculous is my friend Madeleine's birth story. I've already mentioned her and her husband Ryan, and I'm so grateful I get to live life alongside of them and their wonderful family. I'm a stronger and a more grateful person for knowing them. Madeleine experienced a miracle with the

---

52.   Dr. Emerson Eggerichs, *The 4 Wills of God: The Way He Directs our Steps and Frees Us to Direct our Own*. 2018. Nashville, TN. B&H Publishing Group.

birth of her second son, Noah. One of the reasons why this story is so pivotal is because her first son's birth was a staggering three days long! I've never given birth, so I can't even begin to imagine the exhaustion and physical pain, but I'm sure all the women reading this who have are acknowledging Madeleine is a brave and strong woman! So, in Madeleine's second pregnancy, she knew she had to deal with the fear of giving birth again. In the beginning, the fear was so strong that she considered a c-section to avoid another long and painful labor. Instead of choosing that route, Madeleine decided to start a list of things she was going to consistently pray for. That list included:

- A quick labor and birth
- A supernatural birth with no pain; that she would only feel pressure
- That Noah would be in the right position (since part of the first long and painful birth was that her son was not in the right position)

As she prayed these things, the enemy was trying to convince her that something would go wrong with the birth, or that she wouldn't be able to handle the pain, and she actively had to decide to push the lies aside and give them to God. As Madeleine prayed, she felt a sense of peace with having a home birth and encouraged herself with the fact that her body was created to give birth. She had to rest in the peace and direction God was giving her.

Nearing the end of her pregnancy, Madeleine was experiencing no pre-labor. She wondered if it would ever happen, when out of nowhere, her contractions started. At that moment, she began to feel anxious and nervous. She had spent nine months afraid of that moment, and at 6:30pm on September 26th, it was here. Madeleine's midwife, Lauren, was helping her through contractions. Madeleine got into the birthing tub and knew something needed to shift in her spirit to help her body to relax. Lauren, Ryan, and Madeleine's friend Rebecca were all in the room with her, and Madeleine knew she needed prayer during labor. Madeleine said to Rebecca, "I'm praying right now that there would be no pain, only pressure." Rebecca agreed with Madeleine in prayer, and when the next contraction came, it was the worst she had experienced. Through that painful contraction Madeleine knew she had to decide in her spirit that God was capable of taking the pain away. She also knew that even if He didn't, He was praiseworthy.

Madeleine started thanking God out loud for the pain she was experiencing, even though it doesn't feel natural to be grateful for pain, because she knew the pain of birthing leads to a miracle. As she praised and thanked God, the next contraction came and she had no pain, only pressure! Immediately after that she felt her body push. Madeleine was shocked and asked her midwife, "I thought there was a transition before pushing?" Lauren joyfully exclaimed, "Well, there's going to be no transition tonight!" Only 2 pushes later, at 8:48 p.m., Noah Brave was born. Madeleine attributes her miraculous birth to her choice to worship, even during pain. Claiming truth and faith was an important part of the process, but she said the birth didn't become supernatural until she chose to thank God. Ryan, Lauren, and Rebecca all felt a spiritual shift in the room when Madeleine thanked and praised God, and they saw peace fall on her.

Noah is such a special little boy, and his birth increased my faith as well. Madeleine has battled abnormal thyroid levels, and she was told by doctors that she should not have been able to get pregnant. They stated that most women with her diagnosis would have to choose in vitro fertilization to get pregnant because the chances of conception were so low. She was even told that if she did get pregnant, the chances of miscarrying would be extremely high. I love that even with those odds, God ordained that Noah (and Judah) would be born. Another miraculous thing about Noah's birth was that when he came out, his umbilical cord was in a knot. Madeleine's midwife said it would have had to happen at or before she was 15 weeks pregnant, and that most babies don't survive when that happens. God spoke to Madeleine in that moment that if He can protect Noah inside the womb, she can trust God to protect him outside of the womb. My personal favorite part of Noah's birth was that when Ryan texted me at 6:30pm that night to let me know Madeleine was in labor, I prayed Noah would be born before 9:00pm. I knew Madeleine was trusting God for a quick delivery and that she would not be laboring overnight. I was awestruck when I heard the news that Noah was born at 8:48pm. It felt like a crazy and impossible prayer, but I realized that if God can use a newborn baby to increase my faith, He can use anything! I can't wait until the day I can share with Noah that he increased my faith from the moment he was born! The last 3 years, in which she's carried and birthed two boys, have been the hardest years of Madeleine's life, but she has grown more now than in any other season. With all the miracles she has seen, she knows she is where she is meant to be.

If I could only be remembered for one thing in life, I pray I'd be remembered as one who lived life to the fullest because of my gratitude. We all have been given the choice to thank God by intentionally reminding ourselves to be grateful, removing obstacles that block gratitude, and thanking God even when it appears we shouldn't be grateful. Because of all the miracles I've seen in my life, I will continue to choose to be grateful for the life God has given me– both the good and hard things. The more I acknowledge and sing about my thankfulness and gratefulness to God, the more miracles I see. It's such a beautiful journey. What do you have to be grateful for today? What makes you smile? Make the choice today to see those things as reminders of God's love and begin to watch your heart fill with gratitude. Oh, the miracles that await when you praise and thank God through your heart of gratitude!

Chapter 9

The Power of Choice to Return

The perfectionist in me wishes all growth was a linear upward trend. I'd like to just always grow in a way that makes sense on paper. Unfortunately for that inner perfectionist, I've found growth can look more like a rollercoaster than the upward path of a plane taking flight. The more I accept that I indeed have limitations, imperfections, and sin, the more profound God's correction, forgiveness, mercy, and grace becomes. While I'm a much stronger and wiser person than five years ago, my humanity is still present. On this side of heaven we will never follow God with 100% perfection, which means that until we leave this earth we will have a need to repent from sin and choose to return to God. Everyone has had seasons of rebellion or disobedience, and that disobedience is costly. The key to this choice is that we must choose to return to God with a heart willing to be corrected. Yes, this is hard to swallow, but this choice can turn a season of mess into a powerful testimony.

The good news is that the longer I walk with God, the more I choose to trust Him, and the deeper I press into my relationship with Him, the easier it will be come to discern and do what is right. The even better news is that no matter what mistake you've made, or are making, you always have the choice to return to Him. 2 Chronicles 30:9b says *"For the*

LORD your God is gracious and compassionate. He will not turn his face from you if you return to him." (NIV)[53] Let's look at a few biblical examples of disobedience and the importance of choosing to repent and return. Read 1 Samuel 15:22-23 in these two translations, where Samuel is addressing Saul's disobedience towards God:

But Samuel replied: "Does the LORD delight in burnt offerings and sacrifices as much as obeying the LORD? To obey is better than sacrifice, and to heed is better than the fat of rams. For rebellion is like the sin of divination, and arrogance like the evil of idolatry. Because you have rejected the work of the LORD, he has rejected you as king." (NIV)[54]

Then Samuel said, "Do you think all GOD wants are sacrifices-empty rituals just for show? He wants you to listen to Him! Plain listening is the thing, not staging a lavish religious production. Not doing what GOD tells you is far worse than fooling around in the occult. Getting self-important around GOD is far worse than making deals with your dead ancestors. Because you said NO to GOD's command, he says no to your kingship." (MSG)[55]

Saul's act of disobedience towards God cost him his kingship. He refused to heed God's instructions to him about battle. In fact, there is more than just this one act that shows disobedience in Saul's heart. Throughout his time as king, we see him display a cowardly fear of man instead of a holy fear of

---
53. *The Holy Bible, New International Version*, (NIV). 2011. Grand Rapids, MI. Zondervan Publishing House.
54. *The Holy Bible, New International Version*, (NIV). 2011. Grand Rapids, MI. Zondervan Publishing House.
55. Eugene Peterson, *The Message, The Bible in Contemporary Language*, (MSG). 2002. Colorado Springs, CO. NavPress.

God. Instead of choosing to obey God, we see Saul consistently concerned with the approval of people. Disobedience is costly, and Saul's consistency with disobedience proves he never fully chose to return to God. Thankfully, we are forgiven of our rebellion, sins, and disobedience towards God when we choose to return to Him. If we instead decide to continue walking down that path of disobedience, it will affect our freedom and ability to receive miracles in our lives.

I shared towards the beginning of this book that I don't believe God's heart or plan is to punish us when we disobey, but that there are natural consequences to wrong choices. I also believe God allows those consequences from sin to give us the desire to repent and return to Him, and to redirect us back to the right path for our lives. Jonah is a great example of this, as you may have heard. God instructs Jonah to go to Nineveh to announce His judgment of the people's wickedness, but instead of obeying, Jonah runs in the opposite direction. Jonah's consequence was that as he sailed on a boat, attempting to escape the call of the Lord, God brought about a violent storm. During this tempest, Jonah had to be thrown overboard to spare the crew's lives. God would have been justified in letting rebellious Jonah sink to the bottom of the ocean. He had clearly and actively disobeyed what God had asked of him, but God used the consequences of Jonah's sin to draw Jonah back to Him and to get Jonah back on the right path.

In Jonah we'll pick up with, *"Now the LORD had arranged for a great fish to swallow Jonah. And Jonah was inside the fish for three days and three nights. Then Jonah prayed to the LORD his God from inside the fish."* (Jonah 1:17-2:1, New Living Translation)[56] In the fish, Jonah needed to confront his sin

---

56. *The Holy Bible, New Living Translation*, (NLT). 2006. Carol Stream, IL. Tyndale House Publishers.

and choose to draw near and return to God. Those moments of reaching out to God gave him the opportunity to change his heart and attitude. Chapter 2 of Jonah ends with Jonah deciding to obey the call of God, *"'I will offer sacrifices to you with songs of praise, and I will fulfill all my vows. For my salvation comes from the Lord alone.' Then the LORD ordered the fish to spit Jonah out onto the beach."* (Jonah 2:9-10, New Living Translation)[57] Disobedience's consequences gave Jonah the opportunity to be redirected back to God. Although I've never been swallowed and spit back out by a fish (thank God– I'm terrified of what creepy things might live in the ocean), I'm pretty sure Jonah would have classified that as a miracle in his life!

God wanted this return and redirection in Jonah's life both for his own sake and for the sake of others. Ultimately, Jonah demonstrates that sometimes the most loving thing God can do is to allow the natural consequences of disobedience. Think about it: if Jonah was allowed to successfully run from God, many miracles may not have taken place. Firstly, Jonah may not have returned to the Lord and seen the goodness, glory, and power of God miraculously rescue him from the sea. He could have spent the entire rest of his life running from God. Secondly, the sailors that were involved in the story were *"awestruck by the LORD's great power, and they offered him a sacrifice and vowed to serve him."* (Jonah 1:16, NLT)[58] The power of God to calm the raging storm caused these sailors, who were following idols, to turn and believe in the one true God. Without Jonah's consequences, the sailors would not

---

57. *The Holy Bible, New Living Translation,* (NLT). 2006. Carol Stream, IL. Tyndale House Publishers.
58. *The Holy Bible, New Living Translation,* (NLT). 2006. Carol Stream, IL. Tyndale House Publishers.

have known the truth! Lastly, I see this as a loving act of God because of the way He uses Jonah's redirection to show mercy to a godless and wicked nation.

Without these consequences and the redirection of Jonah's steps, this nation may not have experienced a chance to repent, instead ending in complete destruction. I'll say it again, sometimes the most loving thing God can do is allow us to experience the consequences of our disobedience that can bring us back to Him! If I would not have experienced the consequences in my own life, I'm not sure I'd ever have felt the need or desire to return to God. I needed those consequences to be motivated to pursue and obey God.

As we look to grow in having a soft heart, one that is willing to repent and return to God when necessary, there are two different types of disobedience I want to address:

- Active Disobedience
- Passive Disobedience

I share these without judgment, as I've walked through both of them in different seasons. Because of my experiences with them, I can rejoice that God has so much more for you if you're stuck in either path.

Active Disobedience

The first type of disobedience I want to speak into is what I've labeled "active disobedience." I use this to refer to choices and situations when you are aware that what you are choosing is wrong. Active disobedience ignores God's attempts to pull you back into His love. The stories of disobedience I shared of Saul and Jonah I classify as active disobedience, because they knew their actions went against God. My most major season of active disobedience I experienced happened in the time leading up to applying for Mercy Multiplied.

It's hard to share about the messiness and ugliness that existed in that season because I got to the point where I knew what I was doing was horrible, and I hated myself for it, but I did it anyways. For the longest time I felt I had my struggles "contained." They were struggles I thought only affected me: the eating disorder, self-harm, depression, anxiety, and suicidal thoughts. Even though I knew my behavior was wrong, I kept using my coping mechanisms to numb and control different aspects of my life. It was ultimately a spiral of increasing pain and destruction. Let's call some of those things I labeled as struggles what they really are: sin! When those struggles, and sins, I was using no longer worked to numb myself, I needed to add to the list of behaviors. I started drinking heavily, purposefully trying to black out and forget everything. I also started abusing prescription drugs to enhance the numbing effects, and when those didn't work, I started engaging in very dangerous and promiscuous behaviors. Not even including the suicide attempt, I statistically should have been murdered or died at some point from all the risky decisions I made. I knew all these things were wrong, but I allowed the desire to numb and the fear of pain to come before God.

Romans 6 says, *"Do you realize that you become a slave of whatever you choose to obey? You can be a slave to sin, which leads to death, or you can choose to obey God, which leads to righteous living."* (Verse 16, NLT)[59] In this season, I became a slave to sin and I could not even recognize myself anymore. I

---

59. *The Holy Bible, New Living Translation*, (NLT). 2006. Carol Stream, IL. Tyndale House Publishers.

knew God wanted me to deal with the pain from my past, but it felt too hard and scary. There were times in counseling that I thought if I "went there" and dealt with the pain, that somehow the ground would open and swallow me whole. That might sound melodramatic, but I genuinely thought there was no way to face my vast pain and survive. Throughout this time, I knew that obedience would have looked like not continuing to engage in my harmful behaviors. Still, somehow, I believed I had no other choice but to give into the desire to numb. I fully believed I had no choices at all. I felt like a slave to my negative thoughts and behaviors, and depression.

I felt like I had to do whatever men asked me to. I felt I was a victim and failure all at the same time. It never once crossed my mind as a realistic option that I could make choices that would impact my ability to get better. *That* is why I feel so strongly about this book and this message. God has specifically told me there are people dying without this book in their hands, because I'm not the only person who has ever felt like they had no choices in life. Dear brother or sister, I pray God uses my story and message to show you otherwise. He is a God of second, and third, and hundredth chances! When we make the choice to repent and return to Him, and do what He asks us to do, that alignment with His will can produce miracles and freedom!

During my time at Mercy, God revealed to me that the source of my rebellion came from believing lies the enemy had told me about myself and about God. As I replaced those lies with truth, I began to trust God, which allowed me to fully return to Him. In one of my quiet times at Mercy, I was reading Jeremiah 31, and comparing it to several versions of the Bible that I don't normally read. In this chapter, God is speaking to the nation of Israel to affirm that He sees them and that there is a restoration coming. While I was reading and comparing, God told me to write portions from the chapter on a piece of paper, and to put my name in place of where the passage uses "Israel." He wanted to give me this promise directly into my life, and to show me how special and sweet it is to return to our Heavenly Father. After I finished writing, this is what I had written:

This is what the Lord says, "Lindsay, who survived the killing, found favor in the desert, and I have come to give her rest. I have loved her with an everlasting love. I have never quit loving her, and I never will. Expect love, love, and more love. I have drawn her back with my loving kindness. And so now I will build her up again, she will be rebuilt, o virgin Lindsay. She will resume her singing and rejoin the dance. Shout for joy at the top of your lungs for Lindsay. Announce the good news, God has saved Lindsay. Watch Lindsay come! She comes weeping for joy as I take her hands and lead her. I lead her to fresh flowing brooks, lead her along smooth, uncluttered paths. Yes, it's because I'm Lindsay's Father. The one who 'scattered' Lindsay will gather her together again. I will watch over Lindsay as her shepherd. Lindsay returned from the land of the enemy. There is hope for her future. I have heard Lindsay's moaning, I disciplined her like a rebellious wandering sheep. After her time of wandering, she repented, after I trained her to true obedience. Ashamed of her past, she cried out, 'Will I ever live this down?' Lindsay, she is my precious daughter, my child in who I take pleasure! Every time I mention Lindsay's name, my heart bursts with longing for her! Everything in me cries out for her to sit in my presence. Softly and tenderly I wait for her. I am bringing Lindsay back from captivity. This morning Lindsay awoke and looked around. Her sleep had been pleasant to her. This new covenant I have made with Lindsay, I will put my law within her– I will write it on her heart– and be her God! I will be her God, I am her person! She knows me firsthand! I have wiped her slate clean. I forgot that she had ever sinned! The time is here. Lindsay is being rebuilt. I'm taking the deadness and ashes and consecrating her to me as a holy place. Lindsay will never again be torn down or destroyed."[60]

I don't share this sweet word from the Lord lightly. It is incredibly special and personal to me for more reasons than I can express. Like the captive nation of Israel, He also promised to restore and rebuild my life. For Him to begin the process of sweet redemption, I had to repent and turn from my past and sin, letting Him train me into true obedience. I had to return to Him with my whole heart and life. My friend, if you are in a season of rebellion and wandering from God, please consider doing what I did. Look up and write out Jeremiah 31, or another meaningful scripture, and place in your name so that it's a personal letter from God. I have included a blank copy of this passage God gave me as a resource in the back of the book. Prophesy scripture and truth over your life, and make the choice to not walk, but run back to God. Prophesy this over others' lives if you are believing for a prodigal loved one to return. Before God gave me those words, I didn't think it was possible for Him to rebuild my life, and yet here I stand now in a beautiful and precious story. I will never get over that miracle. He's done it for me, and He will do it for you. He is already drawing you in with His steadfast love.

Even if your act to return starts with one simple decision, it will open the door for much larger miracles. A tiny step for me making the choice to return to God before I arrived at Mercy happened on December 31st, 2014. This New Year's Eve was significant for me. Because most of the decisions I made at

---

60. Section created from personal paraphrases and versions of Jeremiah 31.

this time in my life were harmful to my health and body, I decided that I would begin 2015 right by not engaging in any of my dangerous behaviors starting on January 1st. I knew I'd be going to Mercy two weeks later, and the destructive relationships and habits would have to cease then anyways.

The morning of December 31st, I was attending an intensive outpatient therapy group at the local hospital, and I told one of the counselors there it was going to be the last day I put myself in a dangerous situation. Her response surprised me, but also empowered me to take a small step in returning to God. She said, "Let your New Year start today, December 31st. Everyone else can start their new year tomorrow, but begin yours today. You can say no to this risky behavior. Start your New Year today." So, I did. I look back now, and although to some it may look like only one less bad decision, to me it was a choice to take care of my body. A choice to realize I could say no to men and unsafe situations. It was a choice to return to God, and live.

Passive Disobedience

The other type of disobedience that we need to repent and return to God in is a more passive disobedience, the kind that is hard to see on your own. Community is often the tool to confronting this. We all have blind spots in our lives. We can overlook some of our weaknesses, our personality traits, and even areas of disobedience in our lives. It is good for us to ask God to reveal to us any unknown sins we are battling in our hearts and lives, as hard as that prayer may feel. This type of disobedience has happened to me more recently. If you didn't know, writing a book is hard work! Not only that, but any time you are doing the work of the Lord, it is going to make the enemy angry and scared. For me, that is what has made writing this book difficult. I've wanted to write this book for three years, and at the beginning of 2018, God showed me that it was time to actively pursue writing and publishing *The Power of Choice.*

I was excited to be called to put so much focus into something I love... until the attacks started to come. If I had to label 2018 with a few words, the best representations would be: sickness, stress, exhaustion, and anxiety. I knew God didn't miraculously save my life only for me to have a year defined by those words. I'm a daughter of the most high King, and because of that, I know I'm called to walk in grace, hope, love, faith, and peace. Anytime I started to write throughout the year, I'd get sick, extremely anxious, and overwhelmed. Then, I would put my notebook down and wouldn't touch it again for weeks. It felt like an endless cycle of writing, getting sick, and giving up. Writing, getting sick, and giving up. I wondered if I'd ever have the capacity and perseverance to finish this task.

As they say, it's better late than never! In December of 2018, I unexpectedly needed a temporary place to stay. A woman from my church, Carrie, who is also a sweet friend, offered her space. While I was there, we had the most incredible spiritual conversations. Carrie had witnessed some of the different health battles I've walked through; time and time again I would go to her for prayer. Carrie had continued to ask God why I was battling those issues and what was preventing me from experiencing my healing. Then one night, at her kitchen table, she had a revelation. I will never forget her gasp. She looked at me and said something difficult to hear, "Lindsay, you are walking in disobedience in an area of your life!" For a few seconds, I didn't know if I should have been offended or break down crying, but she quickly followed it up with the question, "When did God tell you to write and finish your book?" That question felt like both a slap in the face and a light bulb moment, and it was such a good thing. I instantly knew that she was right. Even though writing kept getting hard with the attacks from the enemy, God had wanted obedience and perseverance. I was astonished! Until Carrie had said those words, I had no idea this passive disobedience had existed in my life.

Since that revelation, I've been writing every week (woohoo!) and I've been walking in so much more joy and peace. I'm grateful for this message God has given me, and I will be obedient and faithful with how He asks me to use and share it. I'm not walking in 100% physical healing yet, but I am speaking it, believing it, and pursuing it. Because I'm making the choice to follow God day by day, as best I can and by the strength of Jesus, I know my miracle is right around the corner. I'm writing this book, I'm listening for His voice, seeking His face, and tithing faithfully, so I know I can claim His promises for protection and healing.

My returning to God after times of rebellion or disobedience has led to the Lord showering miracles upon my life. There's no way I'd be walking in freedom from my past without repentance and returning to Him. In 2018, I felt stuck. If you're feeling stuck now, or experiencing any sort of bondage, I encourage you to ask God if there are any areas of your life where repentance is necessary. We need to choose repentance from both active and passive disobedience. Pray through what He's asked you to do in recent seasons. If you haven't done that yet, it could be a clue as to why you're feeling stuck. Challenging seasons don't always mean we have been disobedient, but if it's played a part, you'll be glad you prayed. Even our disobedience is an opportunity to make the choice to return to Him.

Chapter 10

The Power of Choice to Obey

Obedience– the rebellious side of our human nature does not like that word. If types of disobedience can hinder or delay miracles in our lives, then obedience is the choice that will bring those miracles and blessings. Here's the definition of obedience for you:

Compliance with an order, request, or law or submission to another's authority.[61]

Not an easy thing to hear! But when we look at our faith, obedience is important to God and a requirement to walk a life of freedom. Your obedience to God, both in the big things and in the day-to-day, is a key to unlocking those miracles. The Old Testament Israelites would have been familiar with this idea. The Lord had given this principle as a promise to His people:

If you carefully observe all these commands I am giving you to follow- to love the LORD your God, to walk in obedience to him and to hold fast to him- then the LORD will drive out all these nations before you, and you will dispossess nations larger and stronger than you. (Deuteronomy 11:22-23, NIV)[62]

---

61. Obedience. 2019. In *Merriam-Webster.com*. Retrieved July 24, 2019, from https://www.merriam-webster.com/dictionary/obedience.
62. *The Holy Bible, New International Version*, (NIV). 2011. Grand Rapids, MI. Zondervan Publishing House.

I hate to admit this, but prior to my trip to Israel, I did not understand the importance of that land. I knew it was where scripture took place, but I had a hard time grasping how the physical land pointed to the call of obedience and promises of God. Thankfully, prior to the trip, I was sent maps, books, and resources to prepare for the adventure and to understand its significance. My "aha" moment with the land was when I was reading a traveler's guide. The guide pointed out several key principles from Deuteronomy 11 that helped my perspective:

- *God expects us to love and obey Him because of what He has done for us in the past.*
- *God expects us to love and obey Him because of His promises to us for the future.*
- *Obedience brings victory over opposition, limitations, and obstacles.*[63]

God wants obedience from us, and our obedience produces breakthrough and miracles. We must choose to obey God even when:

- We Don't Understand How
- We Don't Understand Why
- It Feels Challenging or Inconvenient

When We Don't Understand How

Sometimes God wants obedience from us because it is a way for us to honor and love Him. Many times He desires us to obey because He sees where we're headed, and He knows

---

63. Charles H. Dyer, *The Christian Traveler's Guide to the Holy Land*. 2014. Chicago, IL. Moody Publishers.

obedience will bring His best to us. God always desires the best for us, and obedience is the way He positions us to receive it. Because God is all-knowing and we are not, we don't always understand the "how," or the method of how to obey God. This was true for the Israelites, and I believe it's still true for our lives today.

When I think of this promised land and obedience in the Bible, I think of Joshua. When we look at his life, he is found doing what God had asked of him. After Moses died, God charged his successor, Joshua, to bring God's people into the promised land. There are things God asks us to do, or commands to follow that are given to all Christians, but there are also commands God gives to individuals to accomplish His will and plan. Joshua was commanded by God to do some bold things- many where the "how" probably didn't make sense to him, but each time, God led Joshua with words of encouragement, strength, and promise.

Be strong and very courageous, because you will lead these people to inherit the land I swore to their ancestors to give them. Be strong and very courageous. Be careful to obey all the law my servant Moses gave you; do not turn from it to the right or to the left, that you may be successful wherever you go...Have I not commanded you? Be strong and courageous. Do not be afraid; do not be discouraged, for the LORD your God will be with you wherever you go. (Joshua 1: 6-7, 9, NIV)[64]

God called Joshua, He equipped Joshua, He encouraged Joshua, and He instructed Joshua, but Joshua had a choice to obey before he could see the promise of God fulfilled. The Israelites' defeat of other nations and crossing the Jordan under

---

64. *The Holy Bible, New International Version,* (NIV). 2011. Grand Rapids, MI. Zondervan Publishing House.

Joshua's leadership has a clear connection to his obedience. The choice to obey brings freedom, blessings, and miracles. As I read all the ways Joshua was asked to obey, God showed me that sometimes how the Lord asks us to obey, or even how to fight, doesn't make sense. Often, it is even counterintuitive. Does it make sense to go to battle against stronger warriors that outnumber you? Does it make sense to march around a hostile city for days instead of beginning your conquest? However, by obeying the voice of God, Joshua and his people saw the walls of Jericho, this mighty city, crumble before them. They conquered an undefeatable foe. They saw miracles and took another step into freedom.

What about the story when Peter was out fishing all night, catching nothing, and Jesus asked him to go back out in the water and cast his net one more time? Do you think it made sense to Peter to row his boat to the spot Jesus pointed out? How would trying one more time make a difference? How could he see a different result from doing the same thing he just did all night? I know very little about fishing, but it wouldn't have made a whole lot of sense to me for a religious leader to know something an expert fisherman didn't. I must believe that Peter at least thought it was a little odd to cast his net one more time after a failure of a night. The "how" that Jesus asked of Peter doesn't make sense to me. Whatever Peter was thinking, he decided to give it a try and obey Jesus' instruction. That obedience led to a miraculous provision taking place, *"When they had done so, they caught such a large number of fish that their nets began to break. So they signaled their partners in the other boat to come and help them, and they came and filled both boats so full that they began to sink."* (Luke 5: 6-7, NIV)[65] Even in

---

65. *The Holy Bible, New International Version,* (NIV). 2011. Grand Rapids, MI. Zondervan Publishing House.

the moments where the "how" doesn't make sense, when we obey, the impossible happens.

When We Don't Understand The Why

Sometimes it's the how that doesn't make sense, and sometimes it's the why. Madeleine, who by now you may already feel like is also one of your best friends, had to walk through obeying God even when she didn't understand the "why." You may remember her rocky engagement before God confirmed their marriage. As she and Ryan sought out counseling from their pastor, it came to a point where he had to tell them they were not ready to be married. Though he didn't want to dash their young love, he knew God had a better plan for them than to get married too soon. It took Madeleine and Ryan a month to get on the same page as their pastor about pushing back the wedding date, because they didn't see at first why God was asking them to move the date or what a difference a few months could make. As much as they wanted to get married, they made the official decision to change the date. That decision to obey produced both immediate and long-term miracles in their lives.

Madeleine had been looking for a place to rent since she had just graduated from college. She had no job and was wondering how God would provide a place. Two days after making the decision to push back the wedding, Madeleine found a condo to rent. She could not afford to pay the full rent, even with a roommate, and the landlord of the potential place had other applicants willing to pay the full rate. Amazingly, the landlord felt like she was supposed to give the place to Madeleine at a discounted rate instead of the other applicants who could pay the full price! That doesn't even make business sense, but it's clearly God's blessing. Two weeks after the decision to push back the wedding, Madeleine accepted a full-time job offer, and Ryan got a raise at his job! Madeleine and Ryan saw all those blessings as confirmation of their obedience to God. A long-term miracle is that they are still married! Madeleine shared with me that if they hadn't obeyed God and waited, she doesn't know if they'd be so happily married, or even married at all. She knows they didn't have to be perfect on their wedding day, but they did have to get free of some baggage.

Obedience is the path that keeps your heart open to receiving God's blessings. We should pursue our choice of obedience with our whole heart, but I also want you to know we could never destroy God's plan for us. He is always bigger than our sins and mistakes. God loves and invites us into His plans, and He will always redeem our stories if we let Him. Disobedience isn't the end. Unfortunately, when we don't obey, we risk missing out on freedom, opportunities, and miracles along the way. Miracles don't come out of comfort or convenience, they come from obedience in the hard things we don't want to do. Tough obedience is what produces miracles.

When It Feels Challenging or Inconvenient

Three years ago there was an area of my life I knew I had to obey God, but it felt both impossible and devastating to me. The healthier I became emotionally and spiritually, the more I began to recognize how I was being controlled and manipulated in a close relationship. As I was becoming aware of the increasingly unhealthy patterns, I strongly sensed God showing me I needed to cut this person out of my life. It may sound harsh, but the control in this relationship was not only unhealthy and unsafe, it was also holding me back from the calling and purposes God had placed on my life.

Before making such a drastic decision, I sought out wise counsel to make sure I was handling the situation as best as I could. This is an important step. Even with the counsel and support of close family and friends, it was a gut-wrenching decision to follow through with. How do you cut someone out of your life that has been a constant in so many seasons? I was wrecked. I would talk to friends and family members about how guilty I felt and how much pain I was in with making this decision. The pain was so intense and my sobs were so hysterical that my words couldn't be understood. I knew the guilt wasn't really mine to carry, but even in light of that truth, cutting this person out of my life felt like I had a bleeding wound in my soul.

It can still hurt to think about that decision I had to make, even though it's been years, and I am continuing to pray for restoration to come. Whatever the future holds for that relationship, though, I now see the fruit of obedience in my life. A good friend pointed out recently the amount of breakthroughs she's seen in my life since making that painful, but necessary, choice. And she's right. Since then, I've been able to share my story authentically and help others discover and walk in their freedom with Christ. I've been able to serve and give more wholeheartedly. I'm pursuing and living out my passions and callings. By being obedient and not allowing myself to be controlled any longer, I'm able to serve and go and live however God calls me. Even better, I'm free to be who God has called me to be. That is a miracle, and I know God has opened doors for me because of the way this obedience released me to live out my identity in Christ.

An important piece of obedience is that we need to make sure God is the rock we are standing on. Because I made God my foundation and my everything, it allowed me to obey Him in a challenging and significant way. As I deepened my relationship with God, I learned to trust Him over every other voice, and that grew a desire in my heart to obey Him. Trusting God always leads to obedience. If He loves me more than anyone else ever could, and has a wonderful plan for my life, why wouldn't I obey? Now, let me tell you, it doesn't usually feel easy to walk in obedience– sometimes it feels scary and I want to ask a lot of questions– but the more I press into His truth and trust Him, the more empowered I am to obey.

As you obey even when you don't understand how, when you don't understand why, and in the challenging and inconvenient moments, take heart. Know that as we hear and obey that still small voice, we will see God do the impossible in our lives. The choice to obey His word and what He asks us to do creates an alignment with His will that produces great results! He did wonders for those in the Bible, and He still does them for us today. I had to obey God's voice to apply for Mercy Multiplied to become free. I had to obey God's call to move to Nashville, even though it felt crazy, to see Him build this beautiful and meaningful life for me. I must still follow His voice each day, imperfectly but consistently, to continue seeing the impossible and miracles flowing into my life. What is God asking you to do today? How is God asking you to use your power of choice to obey? Take a moment to be still and invite God to speak so that you can obey.

Chapter 11

The Power of Choice to Persevere

Perseverance. What a powerful word. I learned a lot about perseverance when I was training for my first 5K race with Mercy Multiplied. Even in this present moment, I am learning about perseverance. I believe this concept is what ties all the other choices we have together, and makes a lifetime of miracles, healing, and freedom possible. Sometimes God does give us a miracle in one single moment; however, I've found in my own life that miracles often happen when I make these daily choices over time. Running a 5K didn't happen overnight. Some people can do that, but for me, as I've mentioned earlier, running was impossible. Every other time I tried, I gave up. I wanted to just be able to run, to not have to go through the pain and exhaustion, and the hardness of training. Right now, I'm training again after overcoming so much sickness to run an entire half marathon, and let me tell you, I did not enjoy the recent perseverance it took push through several repetitions of seven- and eight-minute runs, with only minute breaks. Even with those increments I only ran four miles, and that's not even close to a half marathon! I wanted to give up so many times, and the only thing that kept me going was pressing into God's truth and knowing this is what it takes to get the results I'm hoping for. Running is hard. Perseverance is hard, but it produces so many miracles when we push into it with God's power.

This year, in 2019, my word of the year is resolve. I have fallen in love with the definition of this word:

"To decide firmly on a course of action" (Verb)
"Firm determination to do something" (Noun)[66]

God has been training and preparing me for this word, as it currently holds so much significance in my life. 2018 was rough. There were still many good things that happened, but again, I'll describe the overall year with the words "overwhelming stress." Stress in my health, stress over my finances, and stress at work. The weight felt like too much for me to carry, spiritually, emotionally, and physically, even with all the self-care I was doing. In the springtime, I was faced with a few very important and challenging questions:

Is my healing and freedom real?
Can my freedom outlast any and every stressor that is thrown my way?
Is there anything so hard that I'd give up and go back to my old life?

I had to walk through last year, pressing into God and trusting Him, to get the answer. And that's where the word resolve came in.

If I can go back to the beginning of 2016, one of the many powerful testimonies I heard was from Joe Beam, a marriage counselor in Nashville. When Joe came to Ramsey Solutions to speak at the weekly devotional that year, I was touched by his life journey. There was one thing he said that I know I will

---

66. Resolve. 2019. In *Merriam-Webster.com*. Retrieved July 24, 2019, from https://www.merriam-webster.com/dictionary/resolve.

never forget. As he shared his life, his pain, and his choices, he said, "In everything, you have the choice to quit and die, or you can keep going and live." I often find myself going back to Joe's words in hard moments. It makes some decisions easy, because there are only two options. Give up and die or keep going and live. That quote holds such significance in my life that I paired it with my word of the year and tattooed it on my arm. Now you can look at my arm and read, "I resolve to keep going and live."

It was as I was finishing 2018 that God gave me the word resolve and answered those challenging questions. God used that year to show me that there will never be anything so bad or horrible that would ever cause me to go back to my old life. Hard seasons will come and go, but I never have to go back to suicide, depression, the eating disorder, self-harm, or promiscuity– none of it! Not because of a one-time decision I made to choose life, but because I continue to make the choice daily. I daily choose to surrender, forgive, have faith, worship, obey, and to persevere. I don't choose things perfectly, but by God's strength and grace I choose them consistently and well. This allows for God's power and miracles to be seen in my life. I had to go through 2018 to be able to stand firmly in this message God has given me, and to confidently share with you the choices we have. I resolve to keep going and live and that is why I daily press into these choices. Hebrews 10:35 says, *"You need to persevere so that when you have done the will of God, you will receive what he has promised."* (NIV)[67] Perseverance is what it takes to live a life full of miracles and freedom. I have firmly decided that this life of freedom is worth every choice I must make to walk in it. To choose to persevere, we must focus on two areas:

---

67. *The Holy Bible, New International Version,* (NIV). 2011. Grand Rapids, MI. Zondervan Publishing House.

- Overcoming Doubt In Perseverance
- Persevering To Your Promise

Overcoming Doubt In Perseverance

I want to share something deeply personal and risky with you, because I believe it's a powerful example of how perseverance opened the door for a miracle in my life. When I was at Mercy, the last thing I wanted to address was the sexual abuse from my past. I thought I might die if I had to speak those words out loud. God, in all of His goodness and kindness, gave me a vision as to what was happening because I refused to deal with the pain and effects from the abuse. He showed me this beautiful, clean, and immaculate house. At first glance, everything looked perfect. But God showed me there was a locked closet in that house.

I purposefully avoided that closet, because deep down inside, I knew there was ugliness I didn't want to face. In the closet were suitcases packed full of junk and garbage; things from the past that were old and rotting. Because I never took the time to deal with that closet, it eventually overflowed, spewing up a rotting and disgusting mess all over this perfect home. I had to go through the motions of getting rid of the junk to experience real peace in that beautiful home. Maybe you can relate, thinking of your "closet" too? God used that picture to help me see that I couldn't keep stuffing away the abuse and pain. By doing so, I was destroying my life. If that's you, dear friend, ask God what your first step to healing needs to be. Stuffing it, ignoring it, and numbing it are not the answers to true healing and peace.

Letting God emotionally and spiritually heal me was painful at times, but so worth it to no longer live under the damaging effects of the abuse. I no longer had to believe I was dirty or shameful. I stopped telling myself I was unworthy. God showed me I am loved, beautiful, and redeemed from everything that was done to me in my childhood. This is true even for the things I chose to do as an adult. It required perseverance and biblical counseling to experience emotional healing. However, on the journey to completely heal from the sexual abuse, there was another area I had to persevere in: physical healing. After my time at Mercy, I continued to have physical symptoms that come from post-traumatic stress disorder. Saying that I was frustrated with my body feels like such an understatement. I didn't understand how I could be emotionally and spiritually free, but my body could still feel in bondage to nightmares, flashbacks, hypervigilance, and physiological hyperactivity.

The book, *The Body Keeps Score*, by Bessel van der Kolk, helped me to understand why my physical body was reacting as it was, and I started pursuing everything I'd heard recommended to experience healing for my body. I kept praying and speaking truth over my body, and I continued seeing a Christian counselor. I even went on an incredible retreat in the mountains of Utah for women who had been sexually abused as children called *The Haven Retreat*. At the retreat I had many new helpful experiences, such as the art of Kintsugi (look it up, it's so creative and meaningful!), drum circles, Muay Thy, connecting with other survivors, and trauma sensitive yoga. All of it was helpful in my journey, and when I came back to Nashville, it was a major answer to prayer to find Abundant Yoga. It's a local Christian yoga studio that offers trauma sensitive classes. The instructor, Amanda, has become a dear friend, and I am forever grateful for how God has used her and her class in my life.

I practiced several modalities consistently, and never stopped praying and believing that my body would be physically healed. While it all helped me, I kept coming back to frustration because I wasn't seeing my body being healed from the trauma. I started to doubt if that type of healing would ever be possible. Then, I met a woman named Ilonka Deaton at an event held by my church. That night it was a women's event where Ilonka sang and shared her powerful testimony. I related to many things from her story. I highly recommend you read her book, *Keeping Secrets: One Woman's Story from Sexual Slavery to Freedom*. After hearing her story, I knew I had to ask Ilonka for prayer. I shared with her what I was still experiencing from the trauma and how I was doubting healing.

As she prayed and spoke words of truth and encouragement over me, I knew the presence of God was there. Ilonka told me that God saw my patience in this part of the healing, and to not give up before the miracle of healing comes. I needed to overcome my doubt and continue to persevere. That moment and prayer gave me the motivation I needed to keep believing for the miracle. I couldn't fully heal my own body. Doctors, medications, or other professionals could not completely heal my body. Ongoing counseling, the retreat, and yoga were all major parts of my healing, and I am forever grateful God used their knowledge, skills, and prayers in my journey. Nevertheless, I still needed God to come and do the miraculous. What choice did I have while I was waiting and believing for a miracle? The choice to keep showing up and doing the right things, and the choice to persevere. So, I did. Rick Renner's February 5th devotional speaks to this commitment to persevere:

Faith has focused desire. It knows what it wants. It doesn't vacillate. It never moves. Faith stands still in one spot. So make your bold confession of faith: "God, this is what I want. This is Your revealed will for my life, and I'm not moving until I receive the fulfillment of it." You must have this type of patience if you intend to beat the devil at his game and successfully do what God has called you to do. Endurance is absolutely essential if you intend to stay in the fight until your enemies are under your feet and you emerge victorious. (Page 138)[68]

After years of patience and perseverance, I received the miracle of healing. As I look back on that time in my life, I feel such gratitude towards the Lord, and I'm in awe of His goodness, and for all those who helped me in that season. My wonderful counselor, Shari, never gave up on me and kept believing with me that God was going to fully heal my body. I'm now grateful for both the good and hard parts of my story, because it's allowed me to have a very real and personal relationship with Jesus, and I've seen incredible miracles along the way. The story of Job inspires me. It used to scare me, but the more I read and study it, the more fresh insights God has given me that encourage me. What we know about Job:

- He had a good life, with many children, livestock, servants, and possessions.
- Job was sifted and tested, and his family, possessions, and health were taken from him.
- In his suffering, he sat through lectures from so-called friends.

---
68. Rick Renner, *Sparkling Gems from the Greek Volume II: 365 New Gems to Equip and Empower you for Victory Every Day of the Year*. 2016. Tulsa, OK. Institute Books, 138.

As I read about Job enduring all these hardships, God showed me that He is never happy to see us suffer, but He allows it at times because suffering, and how we meet God in the suffering, changes how we know Him. When I was in full PTSD mode, I had no other option but to do the next right thing and rely on God for His peace. I had to trust that He could, and would, heal me. Walking through that season of persevering allowed me to deepen the roots of my relationship with God, and now I see and trust His goodness more than ever before. May each season of enduring lead to a more authentic and deepened trust and intimacy with God! Don't miss out on the end, though. Job repented where he needed to repent, and persevered where he needed to persevere. Because of that, this is how Job is remembered, *"As you know, we count as blessed those who have persevered. You have heard of Job's perseverance and have seen what the LORD finally brought about. The Lord is full of compassion and mercy."* (James 5:11, NIV)[69] What was brought about at the end of Job's life? Well, the second half of his life was more blessed than the first, and the book of Job ends with this declaration:

Then he died, an old man who lived a long, full life.
(Job 42:17, NLT)[70]

Thank you, Jesus, for healing us and redeeming our lives so that we can live full and abundant lives, for the purposes of your kingdom and your glory.

---

69. *The Holy Bible, New International Version*, (NIV). 2011. Grand Rapids, MI. Zondervan Publishing House.
70. *The Holy Bible, New Living Translation*, (NLT). 2006. Carol Stream, IL. Tyndale House Publishers.

Persevering To Your Promise

Remember my roommate Cara and her physical healing? When God healed Cara's back, she knew it was fully healed. Jesus had spoken to her that He loved her enough to heal it. She felt the tingling power of the Spirit shoot down her spine, and the warmth of His healing spread across her body. There was a sense of peace in the whole situation. Cara's doctor had previously told her that the muscle spasming could happen at any time due to her ruptured disc, so there was always the nagging knowledge that the ruptured disc could be triggered with even the slightest movement. After that moment, she bravely chose to believe that her back was completely healed. She trusted that God doesn't do things in half measures. Cara fully believed that, and her pastor had taught her that every Word is a tried Word, meaning the enemy of our souls is not going to give up his territory without a fight.

It wasn't long after her healing that Cara was out for a run. The great outdoors was calling her name. With a new back, why not start doing something again that she loved? About a mile into the run, a familiar twinge in her back made Cara stop in her tracks to catch her breath. The pit of her stomach started to sink in despair. Her back was giving out again. In that moment, she knew she had a choice. Cara could either choose to persevere in faith that God's healing was true, or she could shrink in fear, allowing the doubt to steal her blessing. She chose to persevere to the promise she had been given. Cara said she didn't think twice. She started to run again and confessing God's truth from His word: that by His stripes she is healed, and that if He said it, He would do it. When Cara got back to the house, the twinge was gone. That is now over 6 years ago, and her back has not once spasmed or seized up since. She's also been more active in the past 6 years than ever before. Should the twinge ever reappear, all she has to do is laugh and choose to persevere again

What areas of your life are you needing to choose to persevere? Are you believing for healing and a miracle? Is God preparing you for the next season? Are you maybe also training for a half marathon, or a full? I'm only half crazy, as marathon runners say! Whatever you need to persevere in, keep going. Don't quit. Keep living. Ronnie Doss, speaker, trainer, and author of *Leading Lions* once said at a church service, *"When it comes to doing the often very challenging work, I am reminded of the quote that says 'If we do what is hard, life gets easier. If we do what is easy, life gets hard.' Challenge and difficulty are going to be part of your journey, but if you want to grow into a stronger person, you must endure them."* You must resolve to persevere and stand in faith to see God make the impossible, possible in your life. When you persevere, it allows God's power to do the miracle you cannot do.

Since Mercy Multiplied, I've been consistently choosing to walk in healing and freedom. People often ask me if I ever still have suicidal thoughts or feel temptations of the old behaviors I used to struggle with. The answer is both yes and no. I'm glad that Jami, one of the staff members from Mercy, prepared me for this. Before graduating from the program, I was terrified of what would happen if I had any more suicidal thoughts outside of the walls of Mercy. I never wanted to face thoughts of death again. Jami helped me to see a perspective that set me up for success with future temptations. She shared that because our enemy is out to kill, steal, and destroy, it is likely he will attack me at times with old temptations. One example she used was for people who struggled with alcoholism in the past, they will probably face some moments where they want a drink. She said that regarding my fear of suicidal thoughts, it was likely and possible that they might come.

Her next words continue to encourage me to this day. She told me that when those thoughts come, I don't have to run back to them and fear, because I can instead go back to what I learned at Mercy that helped set me free. Those same principles that set me free will keep me free. What works inside the walls of Mercy also works outside their walls, because it all comes from God's words and principles. So yes, I've had moments of temptations or those thoughts from my old life, but no, they are not a consuming struggle that keeps me in bondage. This is because I keep making the choice to persevere. I persevere to my promise because even when I am feeling the opposite, I know God's Word and truth. When I persevere and stand in truth, those thoughts have no power, and they eventually disappear. To persevere to your promise, you must become immovable from the truth, regardless of how circumstances appear.

When you overcome your doubt in perseverance and persevere to your promise, you can enjoy the miracles that stem from endurance. Romans 5: 3-5 says about perseverance and endurance:

We can rejoice, too, when we run into problems and trials, for we know that they help us develop endurance. And endurance develops strength of character, and character strengthens our confident hope of salvation. And this hope will not lead to disappointment. For we know how dearly God loves us, because he had given us the Holy Spirit to fill our hearts with his love. (NLT)[71]

---

71. *The Holy Bible, New Living Translation,* (NLT). 2006. Carol Stream, IL. Tyndale House Publishers.

Let me be the first, the hundredth, or the thousandth person to tell you that you can do this. You can make the choice to persevere. You may need to persevere with your actions, persevere in believing the truth, or most likely persevere in both. If you do, there's no telling what miracles God has for you along the journey.

Chapter 12

Inviting Miracles into Your Everyday Life

As you start to reflect on these choices and walk them out in your own life:

- to surrender
- to forgive
- to have faith
- to press in
- to worship
- to be thankful
- to return
- to obey
- to persevere

one thing you will need is an encouraging and supportive community. Maybe that's your family, friends, coworkers, or people at church. No matter who they are, we are not meant to walk this journey alone. I lean on God as if my life depended on it because I believe down to my core that all our lives do depend on Him. We depend on Him for all our provisions and needs in life, and for an abundance of joy, happiness, healing, freedom, and peace in our lives. This is true whether we believe it or not. Even with that full dependence, we will get discouraged from time to time, and having support and community will help to keep you going.

I love how God has used other people in my life to reaffirm His love and truth when I'm experiencing moments of discouragement and doubt. My friend Madeleine (who may feel like your friend now too) knows me so well that when she doesn't hear from me for a week, she recognizes I'm isolating and that she needs to check in. She always gives me a gentle and healthy dose of truth, grace, and love. In the New Living Translation of the Bible, Ecclesiastes 4: 9-12 says:

> *Two people are better than one, for they can help each other succeed. If one person falls, the other can reach out and help. But someone who falls alone is in real trouble. Likewise, two people lying close together can keep each other warm. But how can one be warm alone? A person standing alone can be attacked and defeated, but two can stand back-to-back and conquer. Three are even better, for a triple-braided cord is not easily broken.*[72]

Our community gives us additional encouragement, protection, and strength.

We will always have a need for a healthy community. However, at the risk of sounding opposite of what I just said, I also want to bring up the aspect of being willing to stand alone. We should never allow ourselves to walk in complete isolation, but sometimes when God calls us to something big, not everyone will understand it, believe in it, or want to continue in community with us. Ronnie Doss, who I mentioned earlier, wrote in his book, *Leading Lions*, that:

---

72. *The Holy Bible, New Living Translation, (NLT). 2006.* Carol Stream, IL. Tyndale House Publishers.

The journey of success is one that we must be willing to walk alone. That is not to say that there isn't a need for support as we weather tough times...but for now it is important for you to know that we can't wait until we have all the comforts of a personal cheerleading squad before we are willing to step out toward our goals. There are times when we simply must do what we don't want to do even if that means standing alone. I have always believed that crowds don't typically travel very far anyway. Be okay with walking alone at times and the right people will show up when it's necessary.[73]

Moving to Nashville was like that for me. I had community and friends across the country who loved and cared about me but were also concerned about me moving to a new city where I had no one. In those moments, I had to focus on letting God's voice in my life be louder than my support and community. I had to balance their words and wisdom with what God was ultimately asking me to do. I prayed about their concerns and what they had to say, willing to hear if I'd been wrong. Since the move was of God, it was incredible to see my community's, friends', and family's faith increase as they saw God's plan for me unfold in a resounding yes. It is essential to intentionally build a trustworthy community around you, but to also learn to trust God's voice. This way, when He calls you to something others don't understand, you will have the faith to stand firm.

In each season of my journey, I typically had a community and a few people that were really in my corner, or on "Team Lindsay." I'm thankful for the family members and people who walked this journey with me, even when it was messy.

---

73. Ronnie Doss, *Leading Lions: 11 Steps to Reaching your Fullest Potential and Changing the World.* 2017. Nashville, TN. Limitless Solutions Publishing, pp 9-10.

When I was at my lowest, many people chose to leave. That loss was incredibly painful at the time, but looking back now I can see that there was an inner healing that needed to happen before I could honestly receive help and encouragement from a healthy community. If you've been stuck in past trauma or hurts and have never dealt with them, I encourage you to find a counselor to help you unpack those messy suitcases you've carried with you. These choices apply to you no matter where you are at in your freedom and healing journey, and a counselor will help you navigate the path and healing from the past so that you no longer have to carry that pain with you. Honestly, most people could benefit from unpacking a few emotional suitcases with a counselor! My inner healing team included counselors, prayer warriors, yoga instructors, art therapists, fitness instructors, holistic doctors, chiropractors, Mercy Multiplied, the Haven Retreat, and a whole lot of Jesus!

Dear friend, on this adventure, there will be joy and there will be pain. There will be seasons of peace, and seasons spent in the wilderness. I've loved, laughed, cried, and have even been in so much emotional pain that I thought I might have to rip my heart out to make it stop. I've stood tall and confident, and I've fallen and failed. There are many twists and turns, and different seasons in life often look nothing like I thought they would. So that begs a few questions: what about when this equation doesn't work? What about the times when we are trusting in God's power and actively using our power of choice, but not seeing our miracle? I can't fully answer that, but I can offer you what perspective I've gained along the way. I think God has us all on a lifelong journey of trusting Him with some of these challenging questions, and things we don't understand. Pastor Mark Ramsey, from Citipointe Church, brought a powerful perspective at church on this topic. He was unpacking the spiritual realm, and how the position we put ourselves in will impact what we are able to receive from God. The mic drop moment for me was when Pastor Mark said:

"When we don't see blessings in our life, it is not that He doesn't want to bless us. We may not be in the right position for the blessing!"

Only God knows the exact reasons for His timing and ways, but we must continue to grow our character to sustain our miracle. The right thing at the wrong time can crush us if we aren't in the right position and mindset to receive it. I could imagine that one of the most detrimental things that could happen for me would be thinking I somehow accomplished that miracle, not God. Or maybe even making the miracle into an idol in my life. Neither of those scenarios would have good outcomes. God doesn't give us good things when we're unready or in the wrong position. These choices I've written about get ourselves in the right position and get our hearts and minds in the right place to receive from God, while at the same time give Him all the glory, credit, and thanksgiving.

If you find yourself making all these choices, yet still not seeing the freedom and miracles you're looking for, don't give up. Even if life feels like it's too hard, too much to handle, keep going. You're probably in a season when you need to continue pursuing these choices, developing a heart that relentlessly believes in the power and goodness of God. As the last chapter outlines, you need to choose to persevere. A hard season does not mean you are doing something wrong, but it does mean you need to be diligent with leaning on God and choosing the right things to open doors for your miracle. Cling to the fact that He is always with you, even in the heartbreak and challenging seasons.

I'm so grateful for my miracles that happened at Mercy Multiplied almost five years ago, but graduating from Mercy didn't mean life was suddenly easy or that I had all the answers. I left Mercy with a transformed heart, not to mention freedom from negative and life-controlling behaviors, but I had to fight with all the tools I had been taught in order to walk out that freedom beyond those four walls. Life was, in fact, very challenging after Mercy. Day-to-day living felt overwhelming at times. I was tempted to run back to my old life and behaviors. There were situations that felt heavy, and I had to make some hard decisions to stay free. The heaviness of the transition from graduating at Mercy into the "real world" didn't mean I was doing anything wrong. It's important to not take that resistance to mean that our victory isn't real. That weight simply meant I had to make the right choices, over time, to live a consistent life of freedom.

Mercy was my major turning point, but friends and mentors who have only known me for the last four years often speak into the growth they've seen in that time. I believe that's because even when life felt hard, I kept aligning my choices with God's power. Because of this resolve, I've grown and seen even greater measures of miracles and freedom in my life. I'm freer than I was five years ago, but guess what? I'm also more liberated than I was four years ago, and three years ago, and even just one year ago! I'm sure a year from now I'll be even freer because whatever hardships or challenges that come, I'll still have these choices and a God that loves me beyond what I could ever measure or imagine.

Interestingly, cross-stitching is an example that speaks to me when I don't understand how God is working out hard things in my life. Have you ever seen cross stitching before? If not, you should look it up to see what the process and finished product look like. You start with a cloth, a hoop, a needle, and a thread. When you are finished, you have a beautiful craft to display. The funny thing is that if you are a bystander, the craft isn't always pretty in the process, nor does it make sense. All you see if you are looking from the bottom is a jumbled mess of colored strings hanging from the cloth. What could that possibly turn into? But the maker, the creator, the person stitching the craft has such a different perspective. They see how every thread serves a purpose, and how every stitch is meant for the beauty of the completed craft.

The same is true in our lives. From this side of Heaven, there is so much that doesn't make sense from the perspective we have here on earth. I don't understand why good people die from cancer, or why immoral people gain a fortune. I don't know why some babies don't have chance to see daylight or why some of the ones that do grow up beaten and abused. What I do know is that I can't stay stuck in not having all the answers.

Pastor Jillian was speaking at church recently and asked our congregation to declare out loud that all means all. What does that mean? Well, Jill was preaching on Romans 8:28, which says in the New American Standard Bible, *"And we know that God causes all things to work together for good to those who love God, to those who are called according to His purpose."*[74] She was pointing out how Paul, the writer of Romans, had suffered many things, yet declared with his life that all things had worked together for good. The shipwrecks, flogging and beatings, snake bites, and every hardship he declared as all working together for good. Jill spoke deeply from her heart and shared that all the things in our life are either from God,

---

74. *The Holy Bible, New American Standard Bible*, (NASB). 1999. Grand Rapids, MI. Zondervan Publishing House.

or He uses them for our good. This is true even if the enemy meant them for harm. All things work together, and all means all. Jill encouraged us to trust that scripture, even when we don't understand or don't yet see the miracle. She declared that God is working on our behalf, even when that work is unseen. God can and will use our broken promises and disappointments. Hear the truth in those words, "all means all." Now, you have a choice as to whether you will believe that or not.

When we actively press into these choices we have from God, He does miracles. Though we can expect these miracles, they often don't look exactly how we expected. For most of my life, I longed and ached for freedom. The journey took longer than expected, was harder than I ever imagined, and it looks nothing like the life I dreamed of as a 5-year-old little girl. Oh but the goodness of God, my friend, is that my life now is sweeter than I ever imagined it could be, even on the hard days. I'll say it again, there is nothing in my life that looks or feels perfect, but it is so, so, good. God has even been showing me that if you would have asked me five years ago to dream up the best life possible, I never could have come up with the life I have the privilege of living now.

Though there are highs and lows, the people I do life with, the places I've worked, where I go to church, how I get to serve, and the goals I have are so much more purposeful and beautiful than I could have ever imagined. Only He can create something so wonderful. I have so much to be grateful for, but the sweetest thing of all is that God and His presence are with me through it all. He sees me when my heart is full of joy holding a baby or laughing in the company of friends, and He holds me when I'm crying and feeling like I've been defeated or have failed. When your miracle doesn't look how you expected, ask your Heavenly Father to give you His perspective. He loves you enough to hold you close and never let you go.

I'm excited for you and the adventure you have ahead. My heart is overflowing with gratitude that we are on this journey together, and that He has given us a path to see miracles in our everyday life. If you are finishing this book and feeling a little overwhelmed, or maybe even wondering how you can make all these choices a reality in your life, let me take a moment to encourage you. Everything I have written in this book took a few years for God to download into my mind, heart, and life. I didn't learn it in one day, and I didn't see it working overnight. Just start with the next right choice that will align you to God's power and will for your life. I'm forever grateful that God showed me how my choices impact the miracles I see while I was training for that first 5K. I'm equally thankful that He used the following years to teach me exactly what those choices are, and how to consistently walk them out in my own life. When you press into these choices, celebrate even the smallest victories and miracles you see, because they will turn into big victories. This practice of gratitude will keep you encouraged along the way. One day, just like I did in the Mercy parking lot, you'll realize that your story is transforming. This adventure is about progress, not perfection; celebrating the journey, not the ending. Let's start using our choices to agree with His power, and we will see freedom and miracles in our everyday life! I leave you with Deuteronomy 30:19-20a:

This day I call the heavens and the earth as witnesses against you that I have set before you life and death, blessings and curses. Now choose life, so that you and your children may live and that you may love the LORD your God, listen to his voice, and hold fast to him. (NIV)[75]

---

75. *The Holy Bible, New International Version*, (NIV). 2011. Grand Rapids, MI. Zondervan Publishing House.

Choose life and blessings. Your freedom and miracles are within reach when you align your power of choice with God's mighty power!

Resources

Truth Statements

Truth statements are a powerful tool you can use to empower yourself to overcome the lies and negative thought patterns in your life. I recommend starting with identifying the negative beliefs you have about yourself, others, and God. After identifying those negative beliefs, ask God what He says about those things, and search scripture to discover what the Word says is the ultimate Truth. Write the truth down on paper or index cards and speak those out loud every day. Over time, God will use that action of speaking truth to create new mindsets and thought patterns. The more you speak the truth out loud, the more it becomes your core beliefs, and it is a mighty weapon to fight against the attacks of the enemy. Here are examples of truth statements I've created along the way:

God is giving me everything I need for today.
God will never leave me nor forsake me. He will never withdraw His love from me.
I am worthy of love.
I am delivered from what happened to me as a child, and the effects of those things are gone.
I am surrounded by God's peace.
God loves me unconditionally and I receive His love.
I have authority in Jesus' name and God's Spirit inside of me empowers me to do all things, including the impossible.
I am nourishing, being gentle, and taking care of my body and God's temple.

I don't make decisions from a place of fear but from God's perfect love.
I am led by God's Truth and Word, not by my emotions.

Jeremiah 31 Confession

Insert yours or the person's name into the blanks for the Jeremiah 31 Confession

This is what the Lord says, "...................., who survived the killing, found favor in the desert, and I have come to give him/her rest. I have loved him/her with an everlasting love. I have never quit loving him/her, and I never will. Expect love, love, and more love. I have drawn him/her back with my loving kindness. And so now I will build him/her up again, he/she will be rebuilt, o virgin .... He/She will resume his/her singing and rejoin the dance. Shout for joy at the top of your lungs for . Announce the good news, God has saved ....Watch ....come! He/She comes weeping for joy as I take him/her hands and lead him/her. I lead him/her to fresh flowing brooks, lead him/her along smooth, uncluttered paths. Yes, it's because I'm ....' s Father. The one who 'scattered'........................ will gather him/her together again. I will watch over .... as his/her shepherd. returned from the land of the enemy. There is hope for his/her future. I have heard ....'s moaning, I disciplined him/her like a rebellious wandering sheep. After his/her time of wandering, he/she repented, after I trained him/her to true obedience. Ashamed of his/her past, he/she cried out, 'Will I ever live this down?' ,............................ he/she is my precious daughter, my child in who I take pleasure! Every time I mention ....'s name, my heart bursts with longing for him/her! Everything in me cries out for him/her to sit in my presence. Softly and tenderly I wait for him/her. I am bringing .... back from captivity. This morning .... awoke and looked around. His/Her sleep had been pleasant to him/her. This new covenant I have made with ...., I will put my law within him/her– I will write it on his/her heart– and be his/her God! I will be his/her God, I am his/her person! He/She knows me firsthand! I have wiped his/her slate clean. I forgot that he/she had ever sinned! The time is here............................ is being rebuilt. I'm taking the deadness and ashes and consecrating him/her to me as a holy .... place. will never again be torn down or destroyed.

www.ingramcontent.com/pod-product-compliance
Lightning Source LLC
Chambersburg PA
CBHW052136110526
44591CB00012B/1741